COMPACT

PRELIMINARY FOR SCHOOLS
SECOND EDITION

WITH ONLINE PRACTICE

B1

STUDENT'S BOOK
WITHOUT ANSWERS

Sue Elliott and Amanda Thomas

For the revised exam from 2020

Cambridge University Press
www.cambridge.org/elt

Cambridge Assessment English
www.cambridgeenglish.org

Information on this title: www.cambridge.org/9781108616195

© Cambridge University Press & Assessment and UCLES 2019

This publication is in copyright. Subject to statutory exception
and to the provisions of relevant collective licensing agreements,
no reproduction of any part may take place without the written
permission of Cambridge University Press.

First published 2013
Second edition 2019

40 39 38 37 36 35 34 33 32 31 30 29 28 27 26 25 24

Printed in Brazil by Forma Certa Grafica Digital LTDA

A catalogue record for this publication is available from the British Library

ISBN 978-1-108-61619-5 Student's Book without answers with Online Practice

The publishers have no responsibility for the persistence or accuracy
of URLs for external or third-party internet websites referred to in this publication,
and do not guarantee that any content on such websites is, or will remain,
accurate or appropriate. Information regarding prices, travel timetables and other
factual information given in this work is correct at the time of first printing, but
the publishers do not guarantee the accuracy of such information thereafter.

Contents

Map of the units	4
1 All about me!	6
2 Winning & losing	14
3 Let's shop!	22
4 Star quality	30
5 Extreme diets	38
6 My home	46
7 In the wild	54
8 We're off!	62
Revision	70
Grammar reference	78
Writing bank	94
Speaking bank	102
Irregular verbs	114
Phrasal verb builder	116
Wordlist	118

MAP OF THE UNITS

UNIT	TOPICS	GRAMMAR	VOCABULARY
1 All about me!	Giving personal information Being at school	Modals (have to, don't have to, must, mustn't, can/can't, should/shouldn't) Present simple & present continuous -ing forms	School subjects Sports facilities School rooms School collocations
2 Winning & losing	Sport Hobbies & leisure	Past simple Past continuous	Phrasal verbs with in Expressions for positive & negative character traits Verbs for winning and losing
3 Let's shop!	Clothes Shopping	Order of adjectives Comparative & superlative adjectives	Clothes, jewellery, colours & materials Places to shop
4 Star quality	Personal feelings Entertainment & media	Adjectives with -ed & -ing endings Present perfect	Adjectives expressing emotion Entertainment
5 Extreme diets	Food & drink Health	Future forms Modals	Food & drink Phrasal verbs with put
6 My home	House & home Places & buildings	used to Verbs followed by infinitive / -ing form do, make, have, go	Home Places
7 In the wild	The natural world The environment	Past perfect Reported speech & commands The passive	Animals The natural world Weather
8 We're off!	Transport, travel & holidays	First & second conditional	Words connected to travelling Holiday activities

READING	WRITING	LISTENING	SPEAKING
Part 2: Finding an e-pal Part 5: Steven Spielberg	Part 1: Emails Beginnings & endings Linking words Punctuation	Part 2: Six short conversations between friends	Part 1: Questions – asking & answering about school
Part 4: The history of football as an Olympic sport Part 5: The importance of team games	Part 2: Planning a story Correcting mistakes A story about an event	Part 3: A talk about a special sports school	Part 3: A visit to a sports activity centre Agreeing & disagreeing
Part 5: Going to bookshops Part 1: Shopping in town	Part 2: Using pronouns Using *who, which* & *where* An article about shopping	Part 4: An interview with two young clothes designers	Part 4: Talking about places to shop
Part 4: Why I love Spider-Man Part 6: Keep calm!	Part 2: Phrasal verbs with *take* *just / yet / already* A story about feelings	Part 1: Seven short extracts	Part 2: Describing people
Part 1: Food & health Part 6: Breakfast	Part 1: Accepting an invitation Suggesting & requesting	Part 3: A talk about an extreme camping trip	Part 1: Questions – personal information, preferences & plans
Part 3: This is what it's like to live in a tree house Part 5: The Taj Mahal	Part 2: Linking words A story about a journey	Part 1: Seven short extracts	Part 3: Giving opinions, making suggestions & asking for opinions Things to take on a school trip
Part 6: Living in Antarctica Part 2: Clubs working to help the environment	Part 2: An article about a season	Part 4: An interview with a zookeeper	Part 2: Describing weather, animals & places
Part 3: Visiting London Part 4: The Northern Lights in Iceland	Part 2: An article describing a photo	Part 2: Six short conversations about holidays	Part 4: Talking about holiday preferences

1 All about me!

GIVING PERSONAL INFORMATION

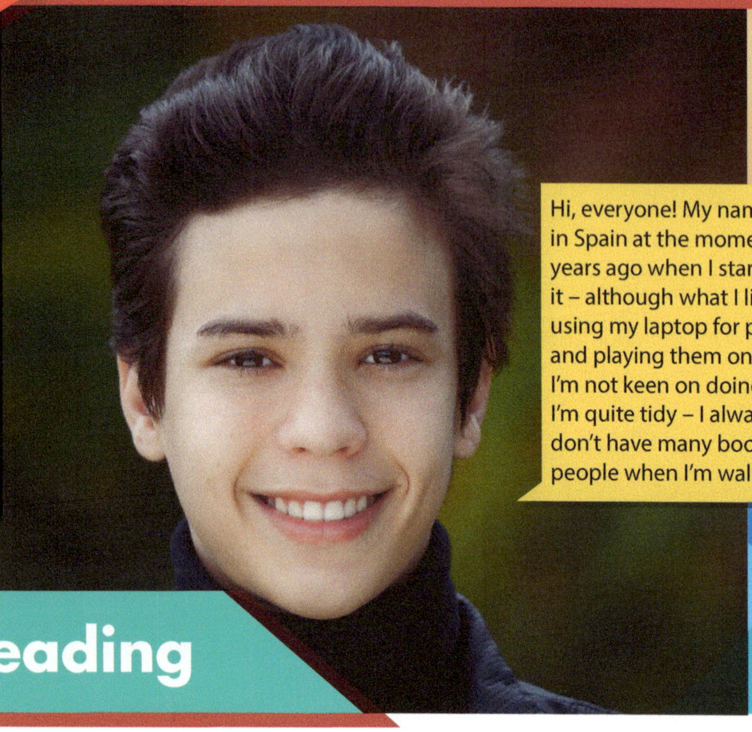

Hi, everyone! My name's Javi and it was my 15th birthday last week. I'm living in Spain at the moment, but I'm originally from Mexico. We moved here three years ago when I started at high school. I'm not great at maths, but I still enjoy it – although what I like best is English. I love watching American TV shows and using my laptop for playing games or contacting friends. I enjoy writing songs and playing them on my guitar, too. I'd like to perform with my friends one day! I'm not keen on doing sport, though – all my friends play football, but I don't. I'm quite tidy – I always put my books back on the shelves after I've read them. I don't have many books, though. I'm also very friendly! I always stop and chat to people when I'm walking my dog.

Reading

Reading Part 2

1 Javi's class teacher wants all her students to find e-pals on the internet – students they can write to in schools in other countries. Read what Javi says about himself above.

2 Complete the information on the right about Javi.

3 Look at the pictures below. Which do you think is Javi's room – A or B? Give reasons for your answer.

I think ... is Javi's room because ... I don't think it's ... because ...

A

B

Name: ......Javi......
Age: ....
From: ....
Type of school: ....
Favourite lesson: ....
What does he like doing in his free time?
....
What sort of person is he?
....

4 Read this information about three possible e-pals for Javi. <u>Underline</u> details which match Javi's description in Exercise 1.

1 Saskia likes sending emails and playing computer games, and wants to talk about sport with her e-pal. She'd also like to find someone who loves reading lots of different books.

2 Conor is looking for someone who's lived in more than one country. He loves music, and is interested in being in a band. He'd like his e-pal to have similar interests to his.

3 Ethan wants to write to someone who's just changed schools, as he has. He also wants to find someone who is friendly and likes animals.

Reading

Exam task

For each question, choose the correct answer.
A teacher in the UK wants her students to find e-pals to write to who come from different countries.
Below there are descriptions of five British students, followed by descriptions of eight e-pals. Decide which one would be the most suitable for the following students.

Exam tip

- Go through each of the descriptions (1–5) and underline the three points that are important for each person.
- Then go through the short texts (A–H) and circle any details which match the points you underlined.

1  Poppy enjoys writing stories and wants an e-pal who will exchange stories with her. Her e-pal should also enjoy playing team sports like she does.

2  Lewis recently moved to England and wants an e-pal who's lived in a different country, too. He loves drawing comic book stories and watching online videos about drawing to help him improve.

3  Amelia's been in several shows at school and wants her e-pal to be involved in the theatre. She enjoys cooking new things and wants to learn how to make dishes from a different country.

4  Alistair loves winter sports and wants an e-pal with similar interests. He loves reading about sports and would like some advice on good blogs to read on this topic.

5  Rosie wants to write to someone who's also changed schools recently. She'd like her e-pal to be interested in protecting the environment and enjoy doing extreme sports.

A I'm **Ava** and I live on the west coast of Canada. Windsurfing's very popular where I live, but I prefer writing about it. That's why I've got my own windsurfing blog where I post windsurfing photos and articles. I'd like to include posts about some other extreme sports, too.

B I'm **Elena** and I'm from a town in southern Italy. I'm pretty good at basketball and hockey, but I'm terrible at surfing! I enjoy reading fiction, especially anything written by people my age, and I love writing stories, too. In fact, I'll send you some if you want!

C I'm **Petra**. I've always lived in Prague, but my family has just moved to the opposite side of the city, so now I'm studying somewhere new. This term, I've joined a school club that encourages people in our local area to use less plastic. I'm keen on rock climbing and I have plans to learn how to snowboard this winter!

D My name's **Ryan**. I was born in New Zealand, but I've recently moved to Australia. At my new school, I joined the school theatre club and I'll be in my first play next month. I'd love some advice about how not to get nervous in front of an audience or any other tips about acting!

E My name's **Ana** and I'm from Mexico. At home, I love learning how to make traditional desserts and snacks. In fact, I've got some family recipes you should definitely try. I also really like performing in school plays.

F I'm **Martina** and I've always lived in the same house in San Antonio, Chile. My room's full of my drawings and paintings that are about nature and protecting the environment. I always post pictures of my art on my blog to share with other artists.

G I'm **Finn** and I live in France, but I was brought up in Germany. Lots of things are different since I've had to change schools, but not my favourite hobby – drawing cartoons from my imagination. I'm also a fan of some bloggers that post short films to show how to draw cartoon characters.

H I'm **Karl** and I'm from Denmark. I enjoy reading about young athletes and the competitions they take part in. I know loads of great blogs about this topic. I like doing sport, too. I love surfing in the summer, and I like skiing and ice skating in the winter.

Listening

BEING AT SCHOOL

Listening Part 2

1 Work in pairs. Look at these words for places you might find in a school. Which of them do you have or would you like to have in your school? What can you do there?

> canteen   classroom   gym   hall
> IT room   playground   reception
> science lab   sports field   tennis courts

2 Match the verbs in the box with the phrases about school below.

> arrive   attend   eat   get   go on   hand in   join
> perform   take   take up   wear   work

1 .... a packed lunch at school
2 .... homework on time
3 .... at school late
4 .... a uniform every day
5 .... classes
6 .... on stage
7 .... hard
8 .... exams
9 .... school trips
10 .... good grades
11 .... an after-school club
12 .... a new sport

3 You will hear Sarah talking about the rules at her school. She says, 'We *have to* attend classes every day.' Notice how she uses *have to* to show that it is essential to do something.

🔊 **02** Now listen to Sarah. What does she say about these things? Use *have to*, *don't have to*, *should* and *mustn't*.

1 attend classes   *She has to attend classes.*
2 good grades   3 a uniform   4 homework
5 an after-school club   6 arrive at school late

📄 ≫ Page 78   **Modals (1)**

4 🔊 **02** Listen again. Which of these is correct – A, B or C?

Sarah says that she …
A always gets good grades at school.
B has her school lunch at midday.
C enjoys playing football after school.

5 Work in pairs. What are the rules in your school? Tell your partner if you like or dislike some of the rules. Use phrases from Exercise 2 and *have to*, *don't have to*, *mustn't* and *should*. Is there anything in the list that you would like to do?

✓ Exam task

💡 Exam tip

You'll hear six different short dialogues in this part. Read through the questions and options before the recording starts. Remember, you'll listen <u>twice</u>, but you should move on to the next question after each dialogue.

🔊 **03**   For each question, choose the correct answer.

1 You will hear two friends talking about their new school hall.
What is the boy most impressed by?
A the space it has inside
B the way it's decorated
C the amount of light coming in

2 You will hear a girl talking to her brother about a concert.
What is she trying to persuade him to do?
A buy her a concert ticket
B go with her to watch the concert
C perform in the concert

3 You will hear two friends talking about the new school they've just moved to.
What does the girl say about the school?
A The rules there are quite relaxed.
B It's changed since her parents were there.
C She immediately felt comfortable there.

4 You will hear a boy telling his friend about problems learning the piano.
What does the girl advise him to do?
A take up piano lessons
B concentrate on one piece of music
C listen to more piano music

5 You will hear two friends talking about a hockey match that the girl played in.
How did she feel about it?
A sad that her team didn't win
B worried that she didn't play well
C disappointed that her friend didn't see it

6 You will hear two friends talking about breaking up for the summer holidays.
What do they agree about the holiday?
A They'll have a lot of schoolwork to do.
B They'll miss their friends from their class.
C They'll get bored before the holidays finish.

Speaking

Speaking Part 1
💬 >> Pages 102–104

1 How do you say these letters?

A   C   G   I   B   E   V   J   W   Y   P   Z

2 Work in pairs. Take turns to spell out these names.

1 S–M–I–T–H
2 J–O–H–N–S–O–N
3 W–Y–A–T–T
4 G–O–R–D–O–N
5 V–E–A–Z–E–Y

🔊 04 Listen and check.

3 Complete the questions below with the words in the box. Add capital letters where necessary.

| are | can | did | do | do | have | is | is |

1 Where .... your school?
2 How .... you get to school every day?
3 What .... your favourite subject?
4 .... you enjoy learning English?
5 .... you got a swimming pool at your school?
6 .... you happy at school?
7 When .... you first start at your school?
8 .... you speak more than two languages?

4 Match these answers with the questions in Exercise 3.

a I think it's probably maths, because there's only one correct answer to maths problems!
b Yes, because my mother is French and my father is Polish – and I also speak English!
c It's in a small town in the west of my country. It's a pretty area!
d I first went there when I was ten – so I've been there a long time!
e I think so. I like my teachers and my lessons, and I've got lots of friends.
f Yes, I like it, especially when I can actually communicate with people.
g Sometimes my mum takes me in the car if the weather's bad, but usually I go on my bike.
h No, we haven't, unfortunately, so we go to the local one in the town for our lessons.

5 Work in pairs. Take turns to ask and answer the questions in Exercise 3.

6 Match the examiner's questions with a short answer from A. Then find a longer answer from B that develops the answer in A.

Question
1 Do you like English?
2 Where do you live?
3 Tell us about your English teacher.
4 What do you enjoy doing in the evening?
5 Tell us about your family.

A
There are three of us.
Watching TV.
Yes.
Italy.
Her name's Tina.

B
She's young and friendly and she makes us laugh!
My mum's a nurse and my dad works in an office.
In a small town called Chiavari.
The grammar is difficult, though.
My favourite programmes are music shows.

7 Look at the beginnings of some answers to Speaking Part 1 questions. How could you develop them?

1 I'm from …
2 At the moment, I'm studying …
3 I live …
4 In my spare time, I …
5 In my family, there are …
6 Last Saturday, I …

✅ **Exam task**

🔊 05 Listen to the examiner's questions and answer when your teacher pauses the recording.

💡 **Exam tip**

To get good marks in the Speaking Test, you need to develop your answers with some detail in two or three sentences.

UNIT 1   9

Grammar

📝 » Page 79 **Present simple & present continuous**

1 Look at these sentences. Then complete rules 1–3 below with the phrases in the box.

I always **put** my books back on the shelves.

We **go** to school from 8.15 a.m. to 1.30 p.m. on weekdays.

I**'m writing** an essay about France at the moment.

I come from Mexico, but I**'m living** in Spain now because my father's working in Madrid for a year.

> routines – things we do regularly
> something that is always true
> the present continuous
> things that are happening now

1 We use the **present simple** to talk about .... and ....
2 We use the **present continuous** to talk about ....
3 To talk about something that is temporary, we use ....

2 Read Tan's blog for today. Choose the correct form of the verbs.

At the moment, (0) I write / I'm writing this blog post. (1) I sit / I'm sitting on my bed and (2) watch / watching TV, too. It's my favourite programme – 'Teen Star'. (3) I watch / I'm watching it every Friday evening at 6 p.m., after (4) I get / I'm getting home from swimming club. I've got a drink, so (5) I try / I'm trying to drink that and (6) I write / I'm writing at the same time. It's not easy! (7) Mum cooks / Mum's cooking the dinner – she's just said it'll be ready soon. It'll probably be a big family dinner with roast chicken – (8) she usually makes / she's usually making it every Friday, as (9) she never has / she's never having time during the rest of the week. Anyway, (10) we work and study / we're working and studying so hard at the moment that we're hardly ever all at home at the same time!

3 Work in pairs. What is happening now in Tan's house? What happens regularly?

What about you? Think of some things that a) you do regularly, and b) you are doing now.

4 👁 Exam candidates often make mistakes with the present simple and present continuous. Correct the mistakes in these sentences.

I'm studying
1 Now I study in school with other students.
2 I forgot to tell you that we organise a big football event this weekend.
3 I am going to the gym twice a week.
4 I'm writting to tell you some important news.
5 I suggest we are meeting outside the cinema.

-ing forms
📝 » Page 80

5 Put these verbs into the correct category. Then complete the phrases below with the correct prepositions.

> ~~enjoy~~ ~~hate~~ can't stand dislike like
> love quite like

+ 🙂	− ☹
enjoy	hate

good .... *at* ....   look forward ....
afraid ....   worried ....
interested ....   fond ....

6 Complete these sentences with the -ing form of the verbs in brackets. Which ones also need a preposition?

1 I really enjoy .... (go) swimming.
2 I'm not looking forward .... (get) my homework back – I'm sure it was wrong.
3 My brother's interested .... (learn) to fly – he wants to be a pilot.
4 I hate .... (cycle) in the rain.
5 I'm quite good .... (make) cakes – I'll make you one!
6 My sister's worried .... (fail) her exams, but I know she'll do well.

7 Work in pairs. Use these words with the -ing form to make questions. Add prepositions where necessary.

> can't stand enjoy good hate
> interested look forward

> Is there anything you can't stand doing?

> Yes, I can't stand washing the dishes after dinner!

Reading

Reading Part 5

1 Read these sentences and choose the correct words (A, B, C or D) to fill the gaps. Look at the questions below each sentence to help you find the answer.

1 My teachers have all .... me to be more confident, which is great.
   A shown   B suggested   C encouraged   D made
   Which verb can be followed by *me + to*? Think carefully!

2 I can't wait to .... rid of my awful school bag and buy a new one!
   A get   B have   C let   D become
   .... *rid of* is a phrasal verb, which means 'throw away'. Which verb do you need?

3 We have an excellent hockey .... at our school.
   A course   B track   C court   D pitch
   Which word means 'the place where you play hockey'?
   Which sports take place in the other three places?

2 Work in pairs. Compare your answers. Do you agree? Why are the other three options wrong?

Exam task

For each question, choose the correct answer.

> **Exam tip**
>
> Read the whole of each gapped sentence. Look at the words that come immediately before and after the missing word to make sure the word you choose fits into the sentence.

Steven Spielberg

The famous Hollywood director of films such as Jurassic Park and Ready Player One wasn't the best student.

Many people consider doing well at school is an important part of having a successful career. However, that wasn't true in Steven Spielberg's (1) ....

As a child, Steven showed (2) .... interest in his studies. But he was interested in film and began using his father's movie camera to record family (3) .... By the age of 12, he'd made his first movie.

Steven's poor grades in high school (4) .... him from entering the University of Southern California's film programme. However, he was (5) .... at California State University but didn't complete the course. Instead, he worked at the world-famous Universal Studios and soon became one of Hollywood's best-known directors.

Over 34 years after leaving college, Steven finally attended his university graduation (6) .... He'd decided to complete his studies because his children kept asking why they should go to college when he hadn't. Steven says, 'I thought I'd better get that degree and get it fast, so I did.'

1 A fact   B condition   C case   D position
2 A few   B small   C low   D little
3 A situations   B events   C actions   D developments
4 A refused   B avoided   C limited   D prevented
5 A accepted   B gained   C allowed   D entered
6 A custom   B ceremony   C occasion   D anniversary

3 Work in pairs. Do you think it's important to get a college or university qualification? Why? / Why not?

4 Do you think there are any advantages to studying later in life? What are the disadvantages?

UNIT 1   11

Writing

Writing Part 1
Pages 95–97

1. Look at the email and the notes in red on the right and answer these questions.
   1. Who is it from and what is it about?
   2. How many points do you have to cover in your reply?

2. Work in pairs. Imagine you are going to answer Sam's email. What will you say?
   1. How can you tell Sam you're pleased he's coming?
   2. Would you prefer to cycle or go on the bus? Why?
   3. What food would be good to take? How can you suggest this to Sam?
   4. Why can't you go to Sam's house after the match? You need to apologise and give a reason.

3. Look at Jake's reply.

> That's great! I'm so happy you're able to come! I know we'll have a good time.
>
> I'd rather go on the bus than cycle, if that's OK with you, because my bike is broken at the moment.
>
> Why don't we take some sandwiches with us? I'll ask my mum to make some. Could you bring some bottles of water?
>
> I'm really sorry, but I'm afraid I can't come to your house afterwards, because my grandparents are coming to visit then. But thanks for asking me – maybe I could come next week instead?
>
> Jake

Work in pairs. In Jake's email, <u>underline</u> where he …
- says how he feels about Sam coming to the game
- says what form of transport he prefers
- suggests what food to take
- explains why he can't go to Sam's house afterwards.

Beginnings & endings

4. Look at these possible ways of starting and finishing emails. How could Jake start and finish his email to Sam?

Hi, Sam!	See you soon
Dear Sam	Lots of love
Hello, Sam	Bye for now
Sam,	Best wishes

> Hi!
>
> Guess what? Dad says I can come to the basketball game with you on Saturday! —— Great!
>
> It starts at 3 p.m., doesn't it? We can either cycle there or go on the bus. It's not far. Which would you prefer? —— Say which and why
>
> I'm sure we'll be hungry while we're watching the game! What food should we take? —— Suggest …
>
> The game finishes at five, so would you like to come to my house afterwards? —— Sorry, no, because …
>
> See you soon!
>
> Sam

5. What is the writer doing in each of the sentences below? Choose a verb from the box to describe each sentence.

> advising   apologising   describing   explaining
> inviting   offering   ~~persuading~~
> suggesting   thanking

1. I really need some help with my homework. I'll tidy my room if you help me. You will? Fantastic! ..*persuading*..
2. It was really kind of you to send me a present on my birthday. ....
3. If I were you, I'd save the money for a new mobile. ....
4. My new bicycle's red with silver wheels – it's really fast! ....
5. Shall we meet at the shopping centre at six? ....
6. I'm so sorry I was late yesterday. ....
7. Would you like to come to my party on Saturday? ....
8. I can't go tomorrow because I have to help my mum. ....
9. My dad can come and pick you up if you want. ....

Writing

6 Work in pairs. Look at these situations and imagine you have to write short emails to friends. What will you say?

You want to …

1. apologise for being late yesterday.
2. suggest meeting your friend tomorrow at 5 p.m.
3. tell your friend about the new T-shirt you've bought.
4. explain why you can't go out at the weekend.
5. thank your friend for an invitation.
6. give your friend advice about handing in homework late.
7. say what you'd prefer to do tonight.

Linking words

7 Rewrite these sentences using *and*, *but*, *so* and *because*.

1. I was tired. I'd been playing football all day.
   I was tired because I'd been playing football all day.
2. I arrived home. I opened the door.
3. I shouted hello. No one was at home.
4. I was hungry. I made myself a sandwich.
5. My sandwich wasn't very nice. I'd put too much salt in it.
6. I wanted to make toast. I'd used all the bread.

8 Complete these sentences with a suitable linking word.

1. I didn't feel well, ... I went straight to bed when I got home.
2. I got onto my bike .... cycled into town.
3. I have to do my homework tonight .... it's due in tomorrow.
4. I remember putting my mobile into my bag, ... now it's not there!
5. .... I didn't have any money, I still went into town.
6. .... the hot sun, we enjoyed our game of football.

Punctuation

9 Look at this email Jennie has written to her friend Robyn. Add the missing capital letters, full stops and question marks.

Hi, Robyn

I'm sorry, but I can't come to the cinema tomorrow because I have to go to the dentist I'd forgotten all about it until my mum reminded me I don't think I'll be home in time for the film my appointment's at two o'clock and the film starts at three, doesn't it maybe we could go on Saturday instead what do you think let me know see you soon!

Jennie

✓ Exam task

Read this email from your friend Jo and the notes you have made.

Hi!
Guess what? My parents have said I can go on the day trip into the countryside next month! ——— Great!
Our teacher said we could do some walking during the trip or try some horse riding, didn't she? Which would you prefer to do? ——— Say which and why
What do you think we should take with us? ——— Suggest …
Do you want to meet before the trip to talk about it? ——— Yes – say when

Write your email to Jo using all the notes.

Write about 100 words.

💡 Exam tip

Remember to think about who you're writing to and how you'll start and finish your email. Don't forget to check that you've included all four points and written the correct number of words.

UNIT 1   13

2 Winning & losing

SPORT

Reading

Reading Part 4

1 How many Olympic sports can you name?

2 Write the missing words.

Noun (person)	Noun	Adjective
(1)	championship	–
athlete	(2)	athletic
(3)	competition	(4) ....

3 Complete these words. Use the table in Exercise 2 to help you.

1 Some of the best ath...................... come from Jamaica.
2 This year, the golf champ...................... was held in Scotland.
3 You have to be a very comp...................... person to succeed in sport.
4 I don't like sports. I'm not very ath...................... .

4 Match sentences 1–3 with sentences a–c.

1 The first modern Olympics took place in Athens in 1896.
2 More than 240 athletes, who were all men, competed in 43 events.
3 Now more than 11,000 athletes from over 200 countries take part in the Olympic Games.

a <u>These</u> included gymnastics, swimming, cycling and tennis.
b <u>It</u> is the biggest international sports event in the world.
c Teams from around 13 countries competed <u>there</u>.

5 Look at sentences a–c in Exercise 4. What do the <u>underlined</u> words refer to?

14

Reading

✓ Exam task

Five sentences have been removed from the text below. For each question, choose the correct answer. There are three extra sentences which you do not need to use.

💡 Exam tip

First decide if each sentence (A–H) relates to the topic of the paragraph. Then look for clues such as pronouns in the sentences before and after the gap to help you.

THE HISTORY OF FOOTBALL AS AN OLYMPIC SPORT

Football was one of the first team games to become an Olympic sport. The first football games were at the Paris Olympics in 1900, but it wasn't a very big competition, with only three teams taking part: France, Great Britain and Belgium.

However, in the 1908 London Olympic Games, the Football Association of England organised a proper competition with new rules. Six national teams took part this time. **1**

The first South American team, Uruguay, took part in the Paris Games in 1924 and easily won the event. **2** The Uruguayan side, which included the first Olympic black footballer, José Leandro Andrade, defeated Switzerland 3–0 in the final. Four years later, Uruguay won their second gold by defeating Argentina in the final. It was becoming very clear that South American teams were among the best in the world.

For many years, only amateur athletes were allowed to participate at the Olympic Games. **3** But at the Berlin games in 1936, this changed and countries were able to include their top athletes in all their teams.

4 There was a new rule which said that the majority of players had to be under the age of 23. Only three players over this age could play in each team. The idea was that it would give African and Asian teams a chance against the big footballing nations in Europe and South America. This helped to make it possible for countries like Nigeria and Cameroon to win gold medals in 1996 and 2000.

Women's football, however, didn't become an Olympic sport until 1996. **5** In 1920, an all-female match had attracted a huge crowd of 53,000 people in Liverpool. In the 21st century, women's football is becoming very popular again, and there are more opportunities for girls to learn to play.

A As a result, they decided not to include football at the 1932 Games.
B Another important change happened in 1992 in Barcelona.
C This was surprising, because it had been a very popular game in the UK in the early part of the 20th century.
D Because of this, they didn't win the match.
E It continued to grow after that and is now one of the most popular Olympic events.
F They impressed everyone with their amazing display of skills.
G The highest score in Olympic history was Denmark's defeat of France in 1908, 17–1.
H This meant that the best professional players in the world could not compete.

UNIT 2   15

Grammar

Past simple
>> Page 80

1 Look at the text and options A–H on page 15 again.
1 <u>Underline</u> three examples of regular past simple verbs.
2 Circle three examples of irregular past simple verbs.
3 Find an example of the negative past simple form of *be*.
4 Find an example of a negative past simple form of another verb.

2 Choose the correct form of the verbs.
1 The boys didn't *like / liked* the new football shirts.
2 We *was / were* very happy when we won the match.
3 Brazil first *won / did win* the World Cup in 1958.
4 Snowboarding *became / become* an Olympic winter sport in 1998.

3 Complete these sentences with the past simple of the verbs in brackets.
1 Layla and Brooke both .... (play) for the school basketball team last year.
2 Max .... (not learn) to ride a bike until he was eight.
3 Jay .... (win) the diving competition.
4 Where .... (Lauren / buy) her tennis racket?
5 .... (be) the ticket for the match expensive?
6 There .... (not be) enough players to have a game of football.

Past continuous
>> Page 81

4 Look at the past continuous sentences below. Which sentence describes …
a an interrupted action?
b something that happened over a period of time?
c an incomplete action happening at a particular moment in the past?

1 It was clear that the South American teams were becoming among the best in the world.
2 While my brother was racing down the hill, he fell off his bike and broke his leg.
3 At 6.00 p.m. yesterday, I was walking home from the park.

5 Choose the correct form of the verbs: past simple or past continuous.
1 *Did you go / Were you going* shopping when I *saw / was seeing* you on the bus yesterday?
2 We *were winning / won* by two goals, but then the other team *was scoring / scored* three goals in the last ten minutes.
3 While Megan *did / was doing* her homework, she *was also watching / also watched* TV.
4 *Was Dan singing / Did Dan sing* when his friends *were arriving / arrived*?
5 When Saskia *skied / was skiing*, she *was breaking / broke* her leg.
6 They *walked / were walking* quickly into the classroom while the teacher *talked / was talking*.

6 Work in pairs. Ask and answer questions about what you were doing yesterday.
1 shower / 7.00 a.m.?
2 breakfast / 8.30 a.m.?
3 study maths / 10.30 a.m.?
4 lunch / 12.30 p.m.?
5 walk dog / 2.30 p.m.?
6 watch TV / 6.00 p.m.?

> Were you having a shower at 7.00 a.m.?

> No, I was sleeping.

Listening

Listening Part 3

1 🔊 06 Listen and tick (✓) the numbers you hear.

1 13th April ☐   30th April ☐
2 1919 ☐   1990 ☐
3 £1.35 ☐   £3.15 ☐
4 2011 ☐   2001 ☐
5 1.68 metres ☐   1.86 metres ☐

> **💡 Exam tip**
> - Before you listen, try to identify what kind of information is missing – a number, a name or another noun. A missing number could be a date, time or price.
> - Sometimes the speaker will give the spelling of a name, e.g. a person's name, a website address, the name of a place.

2 🔊 07 Listen and complete this text with the correct numbers.

Simone Biles

Born: **(1)** .... March, 1997
Became national champion at the age of **(2)** ....
Became world champion in **(3)** ....
Height: **(4)** .... metres
2016 Olympics: scored over **(5)** .... points

3 Work in pairs. Discuss these questions.

1 Which of these things do you think is most important to become a sports champion?

   ambition   family   good teachers   help   luck   money   talent

2 Do you think it is more difficult to be a professional footballer, surfer or gymnast?

✓ Exam task

🔊 08 For each question, write the correct answer in the gap.

Write one or two words or a number or a date or a time.

You will hear a man called Len Bartle talking about a special sports school on the radio.

4 Work in pairs. Discuss these questions.

1 Would you like to go to a special sports school like the ISA? Why? / Why not?
2 What sports lessons do you have at school? What do you like or dislike about them?
3 How old were you when you learned to swim / ride a bicycle / ... ?

International SPORTS Academy (ISA)

For students aged **(0)** ..*12–18*....

Interviews
The interview date for new students is
(1) ....
To arrange an interview, call
Jed **(2)** .... on 0998 354678.

Programme
Students choose one main sport (the ISA is offering
(3) .... as a new sport).
Students must do sports training and
(4) .... each week after school.
To perform well in competitions, students must also learn to train their **(5)** ....
The personal coach helps students with organising their
(6) .... and any difficulties they might have.

UNIT 2 17

Vocabulary

1 Complete the sentences below with the correct form of the phrasal verbs in the box.

> believe in   get in   give in   hand in   join in   stay in

1 I mustn't forget to ...*hand in*.... my homework tomorrow.
2 Harry always knew he would be a champion. He always .... himself.
3 She never wants to .... with any team games.
4 We arrived late and the gates were locked, so we couldn't .... to see the match.
5 Ali's not coming out this evening. He's ....
6 Real champions never .... They fight to the end.

2 Match each sentence ending (1–10) with the correct beginning (A or B).

A   A bad loser ...
B   A good loser ...

1   is polite.
2   is rude.
3   has a positive attitude.
4   has a negative attitude.
5   shows respect for their opponent.
6   shows a lack of respect for their opponent.
7   often bursts into tears.
8   never bursts into tears.
9   shows their disappointment.
10 hides their disappointment.

3 Choose the best verbs to complete these sentences.

1 She *beat / won* her 100m record by 0.2 seconds.
2 We *won / defeated* our match by two goals.
3 They *lost / failed* to reach the final of the competition.
4 The other team didn't *defeat / defend* us because we wanted to win more than they did.
5 You can *achieve / succeed* your dreams if you work hard enough.
6 He *succeeded / achieved* in beating the former champion.

Reading

HOBBIES & LEISURE

Reading Part 5

1. Do you enjoy team games? Why? / Why not?

2. Cross out the verb which you CANNOT use with the nouns in bold.

   1. It's a good idea to work out so you can *stay / get / reach* **fit and healthy**.
   2. It's important to *feel / show / make* **respect** for yourself.
   3. The team *achieved / enjoyed / got* a high level of **success** in the competition.
   4. You shouldn't give up too easily and *admit / ask / accept* **defeat**.
   5. We're lucky to *have / get / make* the **opportunity** to learn team games at our school.
   6. It's important to *supply / offer / provide* **support** to your teammates.

✓ Exam task

For each question, choose the correct answer.

💡 Exam tip

Reading Part 5 often tests which prepositions come after certain adjectives and verbs, so make sure you learn them.

THE IMPORTANCE OF TEAM GAMES

Taking part in games and sports teaches young people a lot of very useful skills, as well as helping them to **(1)** .... fit and healthy. Firstly, games which involve more than just a contest between two competitors teach people to **(2)** .... respect for rules, because no game will work unless everyone plays according to them.

The other thing you discover is that you cannot **(3)** .... success by yourself in a team game. You have to **(4)** .... each other, otherwise you can never win. Team games also teach you that losing is not the end of the world. You will always have another opportunity and you may be more successful against your opponents next time. It is extremely **(5)** .... to learn how to be a good loser because being able to **(6)** .... defeat is an important lesson in life.

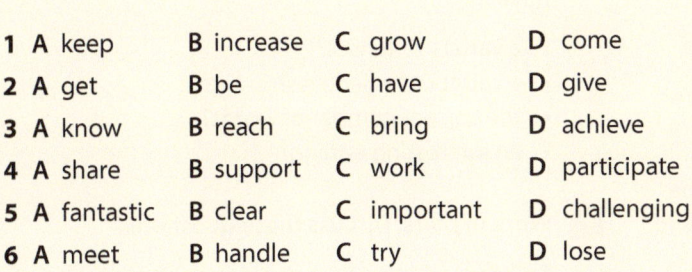

	A	B	C	D
1	keep	increase	grow	come
2	get	be	have	give
3	know	reach	bring	achieve
4	share	support	work	participate
5	fantastic	clear	important	challenging
6	meet	handle	try	lose

UNIT 2   19

Writing

Writing Part 2
Pages 100–101

1 Read this example exam task and a student's answer below. Decide whether the teacher's comments (1–4) are true or false.

> Your English teacher has asked you to write a story. Your story must begin with this sentence:
>
> *It was a sunny day and I was walking home from school.*
>
> Write your **story** in about **100 words**.

> It was a sunny day and I was walking home from school. Then I saw a letter in my mailbox. It's not really a letter, it's more like an invitation card. Feeling curious, I opened the invitation, and on the first page of the card it say 'A Sleepover Party'. Weird, I thought, a very unusual invitation.
>
> Many friends of mine recieved this invitation, too. The only thing on the card is the address, with the time and date. There wasn't a single hint about who it was from or where it came from. But all of us decided to go to the party, as we all think it would be very adventurous.
>
> And so that day, we went to the address which was given on the card. We arrived at the house. It was very quiet around the area. We went in the house and look around the dark room. Suddenly, the lights in the room were switched on and we saw a big beautiful room, and Amy! It was Amy after all! She had forgotten to include her name while preparing those invitations. It was quite a silly thing, but we had lots of fun at the party, all thanks to that unusual invitation.

1 This is a well-organised story with clear paragraphs. ....
2 The introduction is very good because the reader wants to find out what happens in the end. ....
3 The story is too short. ....
4 There is no clear ending to the story. ....

2 ◉ Exam candidates often make mistakes with the past simple. Look at the story in Exercise 1 again and find ...

1 six examples where the present simple is used instead of the past simple
2 two spelling mistakes with regular past simple forms.

✓ Exam task

Your English teacher has asked you to write a story. Your story must begin with this sentence:

When I woke up, I was very nervous because I wanted to win the competition so much.

Write your **story** in about **100 words**.

💡 Exam tip

Don't forget to use a variety of tenses in your story and try to begin and end it in an interesting way.

3 Work in pairs. First plan your story. Look at this list of ideas and decide which information to include.

- Why you wanted to win the competition
- A description of what you ate for breakfast
- What kind of competition it was
- What happened in the competition
- How you felt about winning/losing
- What the prize was
- Other ideas

4 Complete these sentences using your own words.

1 Although I was very nervous, I was also feeling quite confident because …
2 While I was getting ready, …
3 The other competitors looked …
4 You won't believe what happened next, but …
5 The most amazing/embarrassing thing was that …
6 All my friends and family were really surprised/ delighted/disappointed, but I …

5 Now write your story.

6 Work in pairs. Look at your partner's story. Does it have …

- a variety of tenses?
- a variety of adjectives?
- the correct number of words?
- an interesting ending?

7 Work in pairs. Discuss these questions.

1 Do you think it's a good idea to have sports competitions at school?
2 What kind of competition (sport/music/art, etc.) would you like to win? Why?

Speaking

Speaking Part 3
Pages 110–111

1 Put these phrases for agreeing and disagreeing into the correct category.

You're right.
That's true.
I'm not sure about that.
I think so too.
I don't agree.
Yes, but don't you think … ?
I suppose so.
That's how I feel.

Agreeing	Disagreeing

2 🔊 09 Listen and decide which student you agree with: Lina or Max. Tick (✓) the expressions in Exercise 1 you hear.

✓ Exam task

🔊 10 Listen to the examiner and do the task.

3 Think of at least two reasons for agreeing or disagreeing with these statements. Then discuss your opinions with a partner and use some of the expressions in Exercise 1 to agree or disagree.

Football is the best game in the world.

We should have longer summer holidays.

Everyone should play in a sports team.

Girls are cleverer than boys.

💡 Exam tip

Listen carefully to your partner's opinions and use phrases for agreeing and disagreeing.

UNIT 2 21

3 Let's shop!

Listening

Listening Part 4

1 Work in pairs. Describe the clothes you enjoy wearing the most.

2 Put these words into the correct categories.

bracelet   button   collar   cotton   cream   dark green
dress   earrings   gloves   gold   heel   jacket   jeans   jumper
leather   light blue   navy blue   necklace   pink   purple
ring   sandals   silver   sleeve   shirt   skirt   suit   sweatshirt
top   trainers   T-shirt   wool

Clothes and shoes	Jewellery	Colours	Materials

>> Page 82 **Order of adjectives**

3 Work in pairs. Put these words in the correct order.
1. a / jumper / blue / fashionable / wool
2. a / necklace / beautiful / new / silver
3. a / suit / dark-grey / smart
4. a / dress / cotton / purple / pretty

Now describe what you are wearing today.

4 🔊 11 Listen to a girl called Marcia talking about a shopping trip with a friend. Tick (✓) the things Marcia liked.

the department store ☐   the silver bracelet ☐
the purple T-shirt with silver stars ☐   the black cotton jeans ☐
the navy-blue sandals ☐

5 🔊 11 Read these two questions, then listen again. While you are listening, choose the correct answer: A, B or C.

1. What did Marcia and her friend buy in the department store?
   A trousers and jewellery
   B trousers and a top
   C a top and jewellery

2. What did Marcia think of the shoe shop they went to?
   A It was too small.
   B It had a limited range of goods.
   C Its prices were all too high.

✓ Exam task

💡 Exam tip

The interviewer's questions in the recording will probably be very similar to the ones you read on the page. Follow each question carefully so that you don't get lost while you're listening – the questions are in the same order as the recording.

🔊 12 For each question, choose the correct answer.

You will hear an interview with two young teenagers, Zack Walker and Tamsin Lee, who design and make their own clothes.

1. What made Zack decide to start designing his own T-shirts?
   A a present he received
   B a TV programme he saw
   C something he found on the internet

2. Zack managed to put his designs onto his T-shirts by
   A using transfer paper and an iron.
   B sewing them on.
   C drawing them on.

3. When Zack's friends saw his T-shirts, they
   A asked Zack to design one for them.
   B wanted to make one of their own.
   C put a photo of one in the school magazine.

4. Who helps out in Tamsin's after-school class?
   A some older students
   B other teachers from the school
   C parents of the people attending

5. Tamsin thinks the class is popular with students mostly because
   A they end up with really unusual clothes.
   B they save money by making their own clothes.
   C they can show other students what they've done.

6. What does Tamsin want to improve?
   A her sewing skills for making her designs
   B her choices of colours and materials
   C her drawings for her designs

Speaking

Speaking Part 4
Pages 112–113

1. Look at the photos above. Where are these places? What kind of things can you buy there?

2. Work in pairs. Where do you buy your clothes? Use these places to give you some ideas.

> department stores   markets   online   second-hand shops   small shops

3. You will hear a teacher asking two students about how they get the clothes they wear. First read the conversation and decide what the missing words and phrases might be. Compare your answers with your partner, then listen and check.

Teacher: Jake, where **(1)** .... buy your clothes?
Jake: Well, I'm not **(2)** .... going to department stores. I **(3)** .... small shops to big places, really, **(4)** .... they're not so busy.
Teacher: I **(5)** .... And **(6)** .... about you, Tessa?
Tessa: Well, I'd **(7)** .... choose something online than go to a shop. Then my mum orders it for me.
Teacher: **(8)** .... your families good at choosing clothes for you to wear, do you think?
Jake: No, not really – I **(9)** .... it's better to let teenagers choose their own clothes. What **(10)** .... think, Tessa? Do you **(11)** .... ?
Tessa: Yes, I think **(12)** .... – although my older sister usually buys me cool things.
Jake: **(13)** .... ? That's great!
Tessa: It is! In fact, I **(14)** .... borrow her clothes – they're much nicer than mine!

✓ Exam task

 Work in pairs. Listen to the examiner's questions and take turns to answer when your teacher pauses the recording.

💡 Exam tip

The examiner will talk to you in pairs and ask you questions about a certain topic. Remember to give as much information as you can, rather than just one or two words.

UNIT 3

Grammar

Comparative & superlative adjectives
➤➤ Page 82

1 Think about your favourite shop. How would you describe it? Think about these things.

> what it sells   the prices   the size
> Are the staff helpful?
> Does it have the best clothes in town?
> Is it the cheapest / the most expensive / the biggest shop?

2 Work in pairs. Talk about the shop you chose in Exercise 1. Try to give reasons for your answers.

> For me it has the best clothes in town, because although I'm tall, they still fit me really well.

3 🔊 **15** Listen to a boy called Theo comparing two big shops, Taylors and Grants. Which one is better for each of the things he mentions? Tick (✓) the correct shop.

	Taylors	Grants
cheap	☐	☐
big sizes available	☐	☐
fashionable clothes	☐	☐
comfortable changing rooms	☐	☐
good sports clothes	☐	☐
nice food in the café	☐	☐

4 Look at Theo's sentences (a–c) and complete the rules below about comparatives.

a Grants probably has **lower** prices.
b The shorts and tops are **more comfortable**.
c They're **not** quite **as** fashionable **as** the clothes at Grants.

> 1 With adjectives of one syllable, we add ....
> 2 With adjectives of two or more syllables, we add ....
> 3 We can also use (*not*) .... [adjective] .... to compare two things.

5 Complete this table.

Adjective	Comparative	Superlative
cheap	cheaper	the cheapest
expensive	more expensive	the most expensive
fashionable		
interesting		
big		
comfortable		
good		
bad		

6 Complete these sentences using your answers to Exercise 3 and information from the table in Exercise 5 to help you. Sometimes more than one answer is possible.

1 Clothes in Grants are .... than the ones in Taylors.
2 There are .... sizes available in Taylors .... in Grants.
3 The clothes in Taylors are not quite .... fashionable .... the ones in Grants.
4 The changing rooms in Grants are .... those in Taylors.
5 Taylors has .... sports clothes .... Grants.
6 The food in the café at Grants is not .... nice .... the food at Taylors.

7 🔊 **16** Listen to Theo talking about another shop, called C&B. Complete these sentences and the rule below.

1 C&B has .... books in town.
2 The milkshakes at C&B are definitely .... anywhere!

> To form the superlative, we use *the* + short adjective + ... or *the* .... + longer adjective.

8 Compare your favourite shop with another shop in the town. Which one is bigger / nicer / more expensive? Which one sells better things?

Reading

Reading Part 5

1 Read the text and think about what *types* of word are missing: adjectives, adverbs, nouns or verbs?

> My **(1)** .... café is in the centre of town. It's **(2)** .... by the side of the river, and it's the place where I meet my friends after school in the summer. We usually **(3)** .... the kind of day we've had, and we have an ice cream while we're there. It's **(4)** .... the most relaxing place to be when it's hot!

2 Choose a suitable word from the box to fit each gap in the text in Exercise 1.

> best   chat   completely   definitely   discuss   favourite   near   perfectly   popular   right   straight   talk

3 Work in pairs. Compare your answers. Which other words have a similar meaning to your choices? Why do they not fit the gaps?

💡 Exam tip

Read quickly through the text first so that you understand what it's about, before you look at the answer options.

✓ Exam task

For each question, choose the correct answer.

Going to bookshops

What's the strangest location you can imagine for a bookshop? Bookshops nowadays can be found in some **(1)** .... unusual places, such as former cinemas in city centres, which people have now **(2)** .... into great places to buy books. In some cities, there are even bookshops on boats, sailing up and down the river! When they stop, you can **(3)** .... the boat so that you can go inside to look at the books.

Wherever a bookshop is, though, the great thing about going there is discovering books that aren't at all **(4)** .... to you, and amongst them, there could actually be the **(5)** .... book for you to read! Also, if you're having trouble finding something you'd like, then ask the owners for help. They'll be pleased to **(6)** .... a book that you'd enjoy!

1	**A** definitely	**B** absolutely	**C** certainly	**D** extremely
2	**A** turned	**B** prepared	**C** created	**D** arranged
3	**A** climb	**B** attend	**C** board	**D** approach
4	**A** common	**B** familiar	**C** certain	**D** usual
5	**A** true	**B** suitable	**C** correct	**D** perfect
6	**A** point	**B** recommend	**C** confirm	**D** explain

UNIT 3

Reading

Reading Part 1

1 Do this questionnaire about shopping in town. Then work in pairs and compare your answers.

SHOPPING in town

Tick the boxes that apply to you!

How often do you go shopping in town?
- every day
- once a week
- once a fortnight
- once a month
- whenever I have time

How do you get to town?
- by bus
- by train
- by car
- by bicycle
- on foot

Who do you go into town with?
- my parents
- my grandparents
- my brother(s) and sister(s)
- my friends
- by myself

Which places do you go to while you're in town?
- bus station
- department stores
- small shops
- music shops
- bookshops
- clothes shops
- sports shops
- park
- cafés
- fast-food restaurants
- cinema
- train station

2 Look at these signs and notices. Write the correct letter next to each place.

A — CUSTOMERS ARE REQUESTED TO QUEUE HERE TO PAY FOR ITEMS.

B — PLEASE NOTE: drinks and food are forbidden inside this store.

C — Buses depart from here every 10 minutes

D — We regret to inform passengers that the 15:30 to London is delayed

E — Customers please clear your tables before leaving.

F — You may try on only 2 items at a time

G — TWO TICKETS FOR THE PRICE OF ONE on films before 2:30 p.m

Places

on a shop door	....B....
at a cash desk	....
inside a fast-food restaurant	....
at a bus stop	....
inside a changing room	....
on a station platform	....
at a cinema	....

💡 Exam tip

The language used in the signs and notices in Reading Part 1 can be formal or informal.

3 Match the formal words from the signs and notices in Exercise 2 with the correct meanings.

1 depart — e leave
2 request — d ask
3 forbidden — f not allowed
4 regret — c feel sorry
5 delayed — a late
6 inform — b tell

Reading

4 Read the message on the right and answer these questions.

1. Who is the message to?
2. Who is it from?
3. Who do you think Jane, Maria and Sophie are?
4. What is the message about?
5. What examples of informal language are in the message?
6. Which of these functions is the writer doing?
   - asking for a suggestion
   - changing something
   - giving information
   - cancelling something
   - thanking someone

5 Look at this Reading Part 1 question about the message in Exercise 4. Which is the correct answer: A, B or C?

Maria wants to

A make a suggestion to Jane about what gift to buy for Sophie.
B tell Jane about the travel arrangements for the weekend.
C check that Jane still wants to go shopping in town.

✓ Exam task

For each question, choose the correct answer.

1. We DO NOT give refunds for reduced items you have bought in our sale

2. Hi, Sam. I'm in a café with Dan. We're going into Railtons store shortly to choose some football boots. Come and join us! We'll be here till 3 p.m. Jake
   2:34 ✓✓

3. To: All students
   From: Mrs Matthews
   We've just had a delivery of new football shirts. Students wishing to buy one to wear at the match this evening should come to the office at lunchtime.

4. No more than three items allowed in changing rooms at any time.

5. Hi, Dan. My brother won't let me borrow his baseball boots, so I need to buy some. Can you tell me which shop in town you bought yours from? Thanks. Harry
   Tuesday 2:34

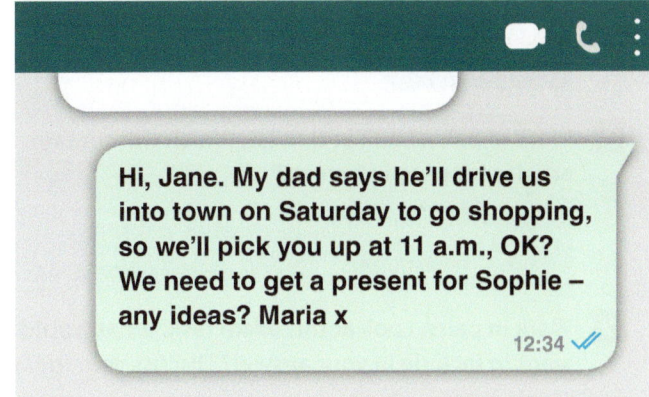

Hi, Jane. My dad says he'll drive us into town on Saturday to go shopping, so we'll pick you up at 11 a.m., OK? We need to get a present for Sophie – any ideas? Maria x
12:34 ✓✓

💡 Exam tip

Decide what the function is in each text before you look at the A, B and C options. This helps you to understand its purpose.

1. A There are no reduced items on sale in the store at the moment.
   B You can't get money back for things you got cheaply in the sale.
   C Refunds for items in the sale have been reduced.

2. A Sam can meet Jake and Dan at the café if he goes before 3 p.m.
   B Jake wants Sam to help him choose new sports clothes.
   C Dan and Jake will wait for Sam to arrive before they go to Railtons.

3. A Some new sports kit will be available for students in the office today.
   B Students are expected to wear the new sports shirts at the match later.
   C The office is expecting items of new school clothing to be delivered at lunchtime.

4. A You cannot try on items anywhere except in the changing rooms.
   B You may take a maximum of three items with you into the changing rooms.
   C There are only three changing rooms available at any time for trying on items.

5. Harry wants to
   A meet Dan in town to borrow his baseball boots.
   B tell Dan which shop he can get some baseball boots from.
   C find out where Dan went to get his baseball boots.

UNIT 3 27

Writing

Writing Part 2
Pages 98–99

1. Work in pairs. Look at this list. Which will contain articles for people to read?

   > fashion magazines   news websites
   > newspapers   novels   poetry books

2. Work in pairs. Look at this exam task. What would you want to include in your answer? Discuss your ideas.

   > You see this notice in an international student magazine.
   >
   > **Articles wanted!**
   > **SHOPPING**
   > Do you think shopping is a fun activity?
   > What are the best and worst types of shop to go to?
   > Is it easier to buy things online than go to the shops?
   > Tell us what you think!
   > **Write an article answering these questions and we will publish the most interesting articles in our magazine.**
   >
   > Write your **article** in about **100 words**.

3. Look at this article that a student called Cassie wrote to answer the exam task in Exercise 2. Did she answer all the questions?

   > *Shopping*
   >
   > *Do you enjoy shopping? I think it depends a lot on where you're going shopping. Shopping centres can be wonderful if you want lots of choice. On the other hand, they're often crowded, which means it's difficult to find what you want.*
   > *I think most people enjoy going shopping for clothes, though, especially if they go to big department stores. There's so much to see! And you can have an ice cream while you're there!*
   > *Of course, you can buy many things online now. But many people still prefer going to the shops so they can see what they're buying. That's really important!*

4. Work in pairs. Look at the photos below. How would you describe the way the people are dressed? Use the words in the box.

   > casual   comfortable   fashionable
   > smart   stylish   traditional

5. Do this quiz about attitudes to fashion. Then work in pairs. Discuss your answers.

   1 How important is fashion to young people where you live?
   A very important – they're keen to have the latest clothes
   B quite important – but their parents may decide what they wear
   C not really important – they're more interested in feeling comfortable than in how they look

   2 How do young people dress where you live?
   A They're smart and well-dressed.
   B They're quite casual.
   C They choose their own style.

   3 Where do young people get their fashion ideas?
   A from celebrities
   B from friends
   C from fashion magazines and websites

   4 Which of these describes you?
   A I make some of my own clothes.
   B I borrow clothes from family and friends.
   C I'm often given clothes for my birthday.

Writing

6 Work in pairs. Read what Monika says about young people in her city. Is it the same where you live?

Young people in my city like wearing clothes in bright colours, with lots of different patterns on **them**. Denim shorts and jackets are really popular, and T-shirts, too. **They** often have the name of the store written across the front. But no one seems to wear big T-shirts and loose jeans any more, like my brother and his friends always used to wear for skateboarding. **He** never wore anything else!

Exam tip
Pronouns are useful because they help you to avoid repeating the same words.

7 Look at the pronouns in bold that Monika uses in Exercise 6. Answer these questions.

1 What does *them* refer to?
   a clothes   b bright colours
2 What does *They* refer to?
   a denim shorts   b T-shirts
3 Who does *He* refer to?
   a Monika's brother   b her brother's friends

8 Complete the text below with the pronouns in the box.

| he | her | his | it | she |
| that | them | they | us | we |

Whenever I go somewhere special, I ask my older sister if I can borrow **(1)** .... clothes. **(2)** .... doesn't mind if I borrow **(3)** ...., which is lucky – and **(4)** .... fit me perfectly! I also go shopping in my favourite shop, where I can get things like inexpensive jewellery that's really fashionable. **(5)** .... is quite a long way from my home, so my dad usually drives me there in **(6)** .... car, and then **(7)** .... leaves me to meet my friends, who love shopping in town, too – when **(8)** .... have money to spend. But **(9)** .... usually only happens if our parents give **(10)** .... some!

Exam tip
A good way of adding extra information to sentences is to use words like *which*, *where* or *who*.

9 Read the text in Exercise 8 again. Underline examples of *who*, *which* and *where*.

10 Rewrite these sentences using *who*, *which* or *where*.

1 I go to a small shop near the market. You can buy great clothes there.
2 I bought a really pretty dress. It was quite like one of Jan's.
3 I showed the dress to Jan. She thought it suited me.
4 My sister liked my dress, too. That was a surprise.
5 Then yesterday, I saw one of my classmates. She was wearing the same dress!
6 Next week, we're going shopping together. It will be fun.

11 Exam candidates often make mistakes with pronouns. Choose the correct pronouns.

1 I like watching programmes *who / which* are about law or about geography and history.
2 I have a close friend, *who / which* I spend a lot of time with.
3 It is a very modern club, *who / which* is near the river.
4 One sport *which / who* I believe is good is swimming because you use all your body.
5 I met a lot of new people *which / who* are very nice.
6 Last week, I went to Zurich to buy new clothes for my birthday party, *which / who* will be in two weeks.
7 I don't like people *which / who* look just like everyone else.
8 They filmed pupils *which / who* were playing football.

» Page 84   **who, which & where**

Exam task

You see this notice in an international student magazine.

Articles wanted!
FASHION
What kind of clothes do young people wear in your country?
Where do they get them?
How important is it to be fashionable?
Tell us what you think!
Write an article answering these questions and we will publish the most interesting articles in our magazine.

Write your **article** in about **100 words**.

UNIT 3   29

4 Star quality

Reading

PERSONAL FEELINGS

Reading Part 4

1 Write the names of three films you enjoyed in the table. Then find one student who liked each film, and one student who didn't.

Film	Name (☺)	Name (☹)
science-fiction film		
superhero film		
comedy		

2 Work in pairs. Answer these questions.

1 Who is your favourite superhero? Why?
2 Make a list of adjectives to describe your favourite superhero.
3 Which super power would you most like to have?

3 Read this paragraph about superhero films. Are any 'essential ingredients' missing?

What are the essential ingredients of a typical superhero film?

Obviously, the main character is a superhero – someone who looks like a normal person but who has a special super power. This is usually kept a secret from almost everyone. There must be lots of action and adventure, but in the end the superhero always wins the fight against a dangerous enemy. It should also include some comedy. ....
If a film is set in the future or on another planet, then it is science fiction and not a superhero film.

4 Decide which sentence (A–C) fits the gap in the text in Exercise 3 because a) it talks about an essential ingredient of a superhero film and b) it has a connection with the final sentence in the paragraph.

A The most popular superheroes first appeared in comic books.
B The story must take place on Earth at the present time, often in a city that looks familiar.
C The superhero film series *Captain America* was first shown in 1944.

5 Read the exam task and options A–H on page 31. Why does the writer love Spider-Man?

6 Look at the first gap in the text on page 31 and answer these questions.

1 Is the missing sentence about Spider-Man's character or his powers? How do you know?
2 Which of the sentences A–H makes sense in the gap when you read the whole of the first paragraph?

30

Reading

✓ Exam task

Five sentences have been removed from the text below. For each question, choose the correct answer. There are three extra sentences which you do not need to use.

💡 Exam tip

It's a good idea to try out each sentence A–H in each gap before you decide on your answer.

WHY I LOVE SPIDER-MAN

I've seen all the Spider-Man films, and when I was younger I also enjoyed reading the comics. Spider-Man's always been my favourite superhero. [1] For example, he can't actually fly, unlike other superheroes.

But Spider-Man has lots of other great qualities. I'm always impressed by the way he doesn't just rely on his amazing powers or any special equipment to defeat his enemies. [2] The stories are always exciting because winning isn't easy for Spider-Man like it is for some superheroes.

I also like the character of Peter Parker. [3] So he has had to learn to grow up as a normal person and at the same time he has had to deal with the challenges of being a superhero. In many ways, he's very ordinary. He experiences many of the same problems as everyone else. Peter Parker is shy and finds it difficult to make friends. [4] He can't tell anyone his secret, and this stops him from becoming close to anyone.

I think everyone can learn something from Spider-Man's example. Even though he occasionally makes bad decisions, he learns from his mistakes. [5] This is what makes him a true hero.

A   Instead, he has to be really brave and clever and it takes a huge amount of effort.
B   This is because he's always telling jokes and doesn't take life too seriously.
C   The most important thing is that he always tries to do the right thing and to help people.
D   He also sometimes has problems in his relationships with girls.
E   That's why most children want to have a Spider-Man costume.
F   This isn't because I think he has the best super powers.
G   Despite this, he finds it hard to accept that his power is limited.
H   He became a superhero when he was just a teenager.

7 <u>Underline</u> all the adjectives in the text and the options A–H. Which ones have a similar meaning? Find adjectives in the text which have a similar meaning to the words in the box.

> fantastic   ordinary   real

8 Some adjectives have two forms. Which of these adjectives describes a feeling, and which describes a thing?

I'm **excited** by the stories.
The stories are always **exciting**.

📖 » Page 84   Adjectives: *-ing/-ed*

9 Choose the correct adjective and complete these statements so that they are true for you. Then work in pairs and compare your answers.

1   I think stories about .... are *interesting / interested*.
2   I get *frightened / frightening* when I watch ....
3   The most *exciting / excited* film I've ever seen is ....
4   I was really *surprised / surprising* when I saw .... because ....

10 Who are your heroes? Why do you admire them? Work in pairs and compare your answers.

Grammar

Present perfect
 Page 84

1 Match these examples of sentences using the past simple and the present perfect (a–c) with the rules (1–3).

a Spider-Man has always been my favourite superhero.
b I've seen all the Spider-Man films.
c Peter Parker became a superhero when he was just a teenager.

1 The past simple is used to refer to something that happened at a specific time in the past.
2 The present perfect is used to refer to something that started in the past and is still true now.
3 The present perfect is used to talk about past experiences when the time is not stated, often with *ever* and *never*.

2 Look at these examples of other uses of the present perfect. Choose the correct phrases in the explanations.

1 *The news has finished. You can watch your programme now.*
The person is talking about something which happened *very recently / a long time ago*.

2 *I've watched three films this morning and it's still only 11 a.m.!*
The person is speaking about a time period which *has / hasn't* finished.

3 Complete these sentences with *has, have, has not* or *have not*. In which sentence can you NOT use contractions (*'s / 've / hasn't / haven't*)?

1 .... you ever seen *Star Wars*?
2 My mother .... never watched a scary film.
3 We .... been to see the new comedy. It was great!
4 My teacher .... told us to watch a film in English for homework. I'm going to watch *Toy Story*.
5 My brother .... bought a new DVD for ages. He usually buys one every month.
6 I'm so sorry. I .... given you the money for the tickets you bought.

4 Look at these examples of the present perfect with *for* and *since*. Then complete the sentences below so that they are true for you.

*I've been at school **since** 8 a.m.*
*I've been at school **for** six hours.*

1 I've lived in my house/flat for ....
2 I've studied English since ....
3 I haven't eaten anything for ....
4 I haven't been to the cinema since ....
5 I've known my best friend since ....
6 I haven't bought a new book for ....

5 👁 Exam candidates often make mistakes with the present perfect. Choose the correct form of the verbs in these sentences.

1 My best friend's name is Ola. I *know / I've known* her since I was three.
2 They *live / have lived* there since 1995.
3 Last summer, I *have met / met* a boy called Roberto in Venice.
4 I *lost / I've lost* my sunglasses during the school trip to Milan two weeks ago.
5 I hope I *help / have helped* you.

6 Put these words in the correct order to make questions. Then ask and answer in pairs.

1 watched / many / How / films / you / have / week / this / ?
2 this / cinema / How / you / been / times / have / the / to / month / many / ?
3 language / in / ever / you / Have / a / seen / film / another / ?
4 film / seen / more / times / five / than / you / Which / have / ?
5 cried / ever / you / watching / while / film / a / Have / ?
6 scariest / seen / ever / What's / you / the / film / have / ?

32

Reading

Reading Part 6

1 Put the adjectives in the box into the correct categories.
Sometimes adjectives can go with more than one preposition.

afraid   amazed   annoyed   anxious   disappointed   excited
impressed   jealous   satisfied   serious   surprised   worried

of	about	by	with

2 Work in pairs. Discuss these questions.

1 Have you ever been jealous of anyone?
2 Have you been excited about anything recently?
3 Have you been annoyed by anyone or anything recently?

3 Decide what kind of word is missing from these statements: a preposition, a linking word or a comparative form. Then complete the gaps.

1 Talking in front of an audience is .... frightening than taking an exam.
2 Some people never get nervous .... doing anything.
3 Feeling anxious is a good thing .... it helps people to perform better.

4 Work in pairs. Decide if you agree with the statements in Exercise 3.

✓ Exam task

For each question, write the correct answer.
Write one word for each gap.

💡 Exam tip

Read the whole sentence and decide what part of speech the missing word is, e.g. verb, article, etc.

KEEP CALM!

If you get really nervous when you have to perform in front of an audience, you're not alone. It's a very common fear. Even some very experienced actors and musicians get extremely anxious before performing. Some people say that feeling anxious makes **(1)** .... give a better performance, but other people can feel **(2)** .... nervous that they can't perform at all. This is a very serious problem **(3)** .... it affects their confidence and can destroy their career.

The **(4)** .... useful thing to do if you feel worried about a performance is to try to relax. Don't think about all the things that could go wrong. Instead, keep calm and think positively. Before the performance, imagine the audience clapping and laughing. Think about **(5)** .... good you'll feel after a successful performance. And remember, if you make a **(6)** .... mistakes, the audience probably won't even notice.

5 What makes you nervous? How do you try to deal with it?

Listening

Listening Part 1

1. Look at the pictures for questions 1–7 in the exam task. Can you name all the things? Practise saying the numbers.
2. Look at the questions in the exam task. <u>Underline</u> the key words.

> **Exam tip**
> You must listen very carefully because all of the things in the pictures are usually mentioned, but only one picture is correct.

Exam task

🔊 17 For each question, choose the correct answer.

1 What time does the film start?

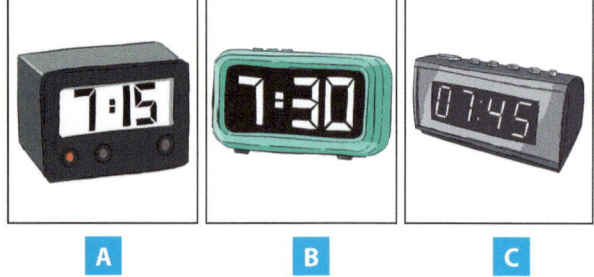

2 What did Jenny buy at the film festival?

3 Which instrument has the boy recently started learning?

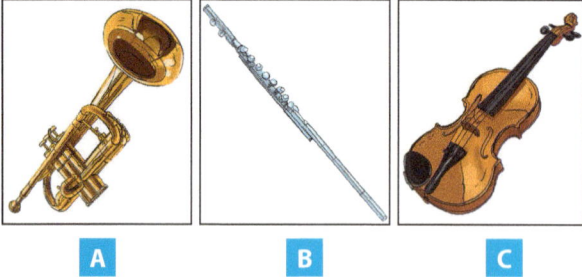

4 How did the family travel to the concert?

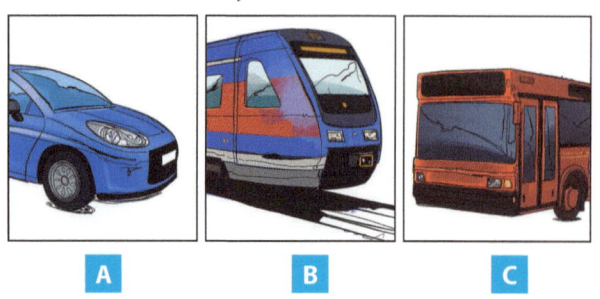

5 Which circus tickets did the man decide to buy?

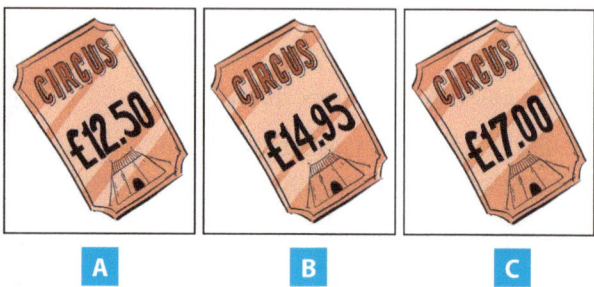

6 What do the speakers decide to watch on TV?

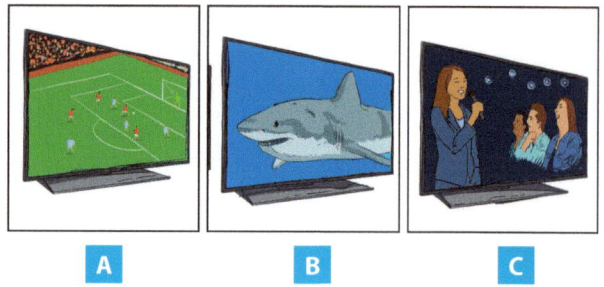

7 Who do the speakers think will win the singing competition?

Speaking

Speaking Part 2
Pages 105–109

1 🔊 **18** Listen to Marco describing the people in the photo below. What is he describing?

A their clothes
B what they are saying
C their actions

2 What does Marco say when he doesn't know a word?

3 Complete Marco's sentences.

1 The people .... very excited.
2 It .... a special day.

4 Choose the correct form of the verbs.

1 In this photo, I *can see / am seeing* …
2 In this photo, there *is / are* a family …
3 The woman in the photo *plays / is playing* the guitar.
4 I think this photo *is / was* taken in India.
5 There are some people who *walk / are walking* in the park.
6 The man *wears / is wearing* shorts.
7 I think the woman *is / looks* a teacher.
8 It *looks / is looking* like a very peaceful place.

> 💡 **Exam tip**
> If you don't know a word for something, try to describe it in another way with different words. You can improve your marks by doing this.

✅ **Exam task**

Work in pairs. Describe what you can see in the photos. Use the language in Exercises 2–4.

Student A: Describe photo 1.

Student B: Describe photo 2.

Try to include as many details as you can about …

- the people: how they're feeling, their clothes, their age, what they're doing, what they look like
- the place: what kind of place it is, which country it could be, what the weather is like, what the occasion is.

Photo 1

Photo 2

Writing

Writing Part 2
>> Pages 100–101

1 Look at the example exam task. Read a student's answer below and answer these questions.

1 Do you think it's a good story? Why? / Why not?
2 What kind of person is Lisa?

Your English teacher has asked you to write a story.
Your story must begin with this sentence:

The best day of Lisa's life started as soon as she got on the bus.

Write your **story** in about **100 words**.

The best day of Lisa's life started as soon as she got on the bus. <u>Lisa</u> wanted to be a singer and she saw a famous pop star on the bus. So Lisa asked her, '<u>How can I be a singer.</u> The woman said, 'There is no secret about being a singer, <u>just</u> work.' Lisa thought she <u>has had</u> a great voice and she studied all the time. When she was <u>still</u> young she <u>joined in a talent show</u> in America. She didn't win, <u>but</u> she was second, <u>but</u> Lisa never gave up and one year later she <u>joined another talent show</u>. This time Lisa won the <u>competetion</u>. Five years later, Lisa was a singer and she was so happy.

2 Look at these notes the teacher made. Match them with the <u>underlined</u> mistakes in the student's answer. Then try to correct them.

1 This verb doesn't collocate with the noun (x2). Which phrasal verb can you use instead?
2 Wrong spelling
3 Use a pronoun instead of repeating this word.
4 Use a different adverb here.
5 Wrong tense
6 Add an adverb here.
7 Wrong punctuation at the end of this sentence.
8 Avoid using the same linking word twice in a sentence.

Phrasal verbs with *take*

3 Complete these sentences with the correct form of the phrasal verbs in brackets.

1 Sarah .... (take up) singing when she was ten years old.
2 Since then, she .... (take part) in lots of competitions.
3 The last competition .... (take place) in a big theatre.

4 Discuss these questions in pairs.

1 Which is the most popular singing competition on TV in your country?
2 Why do you think singing competitions are popular?
3 Would you take part in a TV competition? Why? / Why not?
4 Which new hobby would you like to take up? Have you ever taken up a new hobby and then quickly given it up?

Writing

>> Page 85 *ever, never, yet, already & just / since & for*

5 Look at the underlined words in sentences 1–3. Then match the sentences with definitions a–c.

1 I've just finished my homework.
2 I haven't done my homework yet.
3 I've already finished my homework.

a This word is used to emphasise that something has happened sooner than expected.
b This word is used to emphasise that something has happened a few moments ago.
c This word is used to show that the speaker intends to complete an action or do something, but hasn't started it.

6 Look at the photo and use your imagination to complete these sentences.

1 The girls in the photo have already ....
2 They haven't .... yet.
3 They've just ....

7 Choose the correct words.

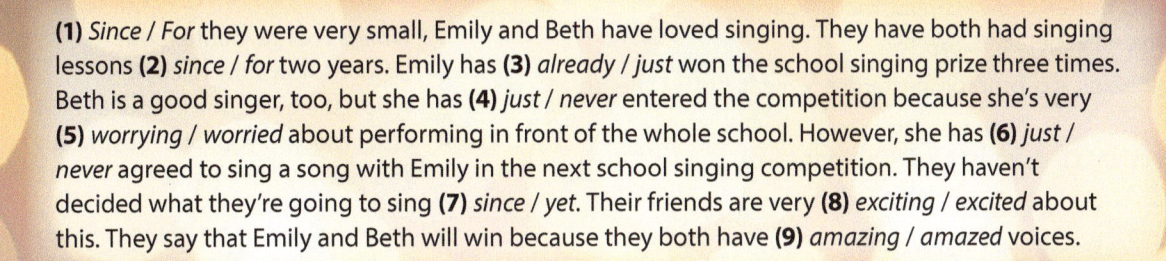

(1) *Since / For* they were very small, Emily and Beth have loved singing. They have both had singing lessons (2) *since / for* two years. Emily has (3) *already / just* won the school singing prize three times. Beth is a good singer, too, but she has (4) *just / never* entered the competition because she's very (5) *worrying / worried* about performing in front of the whole school. However, she has (6) *just / never* agreed to sing a song with Emily in the next school singing competition. They haven't decided what they're going to sing (7) *since / yet*. Their friends are very (8) *exciting / excited* about this. They say that Emily and Beth will win because they both have (9) *amazing / amazed* voices.

✓ Exam task

Your English teacher has asked you to write a story.
Your story must begin with this sentence:

When he read the message from his friend, Matthew felt both excited and very nervous.

Write your **story** in about **100 words**.

💡 Exam tip

Try to include at least two different adjectives, two different tenses, two different linking words and several different verbs (including a phrasal verb if possible) in your writing.

8 Check your story for spelling and punctuation mistakes.

5 Extreme diets

FOOD & DRINK

A Sara Harvey: marathon runner

B Lee Martin: polar scientist

C Karen Curtis: jockey

Vocabulary

1 Look at the photos. What might these people eat before a race or an expedition? Match the people (A–C) with the foods you think they often/never eat (1–3).

	Often	Never
1	fruit, yoghurt, fish, salad	fried food, eggs
2	biscuits, soup, butter, cheese, bread, fried sausages, frozen vegetables, raw fish	salad
3	boiled vegetables, e.g. broccoli, pasta/rice	meat, butter, cheese

2 Match the adjectives (1–4) with the definitions (a–d).

1 frozen   a uncooked
2 raw   b cooked in hot water
3 fried   c very cold
4 boiled   d cooked in oil

3 Complete the questions below with the words in the box. Then ask and answer in pairs.

> fit   fitness   health   healthiest   unfit   unhealthy

1 Which person do you think has the .... diet?
2 Which of the foods in Exercise 1 are good for your .... ?
3 Which person do you think has to do the most .... training?
4 Which person often eats .... food like biscuits?
5 Which person's diet could make them weak and .... ?
6 Which person has to put on weight to keep .... and strong?

4 Put each food into the correct category in the table on the right.

> beef   cabbage   carrot   chicken   cod   corn
> grape   lamb   lettuce   peach   pineapple
> salmon   spinach   strawberry   tuna   turkey

5 Can you add two words to each group in Exercise 4? Which of these foods do you like/dislike?

6 Match the questions (1–4) with the answers (a–d). Then ask and answer in pairs.

1 What's your favourite food?
2 Do you know how to cook?
3 Who's the best cook in your family?
4 What food do you miss most when you're away from home?

a My mum does most of the cooking and she can cook all kinds of food really well. But my dad is very good at barbecues. He does the best steaks. So both my parents can cook very well.
b I can only make fried eggs. I've tried making cakes, but they're not very good.
c When I'm staying at a friend's house or when I'm on holiday, I can't wait to get home and have some of the bread my grandmother makes. It's really good.
d I like all kinds of food, but I definitely couldn't live without chocolate.

Fruit	Vegetables	Fish	Meat

Listening

Listening Part 3

1 Complete the sentences below with the words and numbers in the box. You can put two words or numbers in each gap.

| chips | a fried egg | 53 | 2007 | fruit | 50 | ice cream | knee | shoulder | 2009 |

1 The first time Karen took part in a horse race was in .... / ....
2 Karen misses eating .... / ....
3 Karen weighs .... / .... kg at the moment.
4 For breakfast, Karen has .... / .... and a slice of toast.
5 Karen broke her .... / .... about two years ago.

2 🔊 19 Listen to Karen and circle the correct words/numbers in the sentences in Exercise 1.

3 🔊 20 Look at these sentences about Lee Martin. Think of possible words to fit in the gaps. Then listen and see if you were correct.

1 Lee often spends .... days camping on the ice.
2 He's suffered from sore ....
3 He says it's often difficult to make hot food because of the ....
4 He never eats ....
5 The food he says he really misses when he is in Antarctica is ....

✓ Exam task

🔊 21 For each question, write the correct answer in the gap. Write one or two words or a number or a date or a time.

You will hear a man called Tony James giving a talk about an extreme camping trip.

💡 Exam tip
In Listening Part 3, you'll often hear two words which could possibly be the answer, but only one will be correct.

EXTREME CAMPING TRIP

Training day: (1) ....

Food
Plenty of raw food available.
You will learn where to find (2) ....
(3) .... can be quite tasty.
No (4) .... on this trip because it's difficult and takes too long.

Cooking
You will learn how to use a (5) .... to cook food on.
It's important to (6) .... from rivers and streams.

4 Would you like to go on an extreme camping trip like the one Tony James talks about? Why? / Why not?

UNIT 5

Grammar

Future forms
Page 86

1 Look at the underlined verb forms and answer the questions below each sentence.

1 'We're going on holiday next week. We're staying at a campsite near a lake.'
Is Tom talking about the present or future? Is this an arrangement?

2 'I hope the weather will be good.'
Is Tom talking about the present or future? Is this something he knows will happen?

3 'I'm going to catch a big fish to cook on the barbecue.'
Is Tom talking about the present or future? Is this something he plans to do?

4 'We're going to buy a new tent tomorrow.'
Is Tom talking about the present or future? Is this something the family have already decided to do?

5 'I'll phone you when I get back from camping.'
Is Tom talking about the present or future? Is this a promise or an arrangement?

2 Complete these rules with *the present continuous, the present simple, be going to* or *will*.

1 We use .... + infinitive to make predictions about the future (often after verbs such as *hope, expect, think*) and for promises or for making decisions or offers at the time of speaking.

2 We use .... + infinitive to talk about future plans and intentions.

3 We use .... to talk about future arrangements.

4 We can use .... with a future meaning, but only to talk about timetables in the future.

3 Choose the correct form of the verbs to complete these dialogues.

1 **A:** I'm sure *you'll love / you're loving* eating insects.
   B: I hope you're right!
2 **A:** Can you give this book to Ellis?
   B: No problem. *I see / I'm seeing* him tomorrow.
3 **A:** I'm really hungry.
   B: *I'll make / I make* you a sandwich.
4 **A:** What time is your exam tomorrow?
   B: It *will start / starts* at 9.00 a.m.
5 **A:** I don't know what topic to do for my essay.
   B: Don't you? *I'll do / I'm going to do* mine on famous polar scientists.
6 **A:** *We're driving / We'll drive* all round Spain for our holiday this year.
   B: Really? Where *are you going / do you go* first?
7 **A:** Please hurry, *we're missing / we're going to miss* the bus. It *leaves / will leave* in five minutes!
   B: Don't worry, *we'll get / we're going to get* there on time.

4 Complete these questions with *is, are* or *will*. Then ask and answer in pairs.

1 What .... you having for dinner this evening?
2 Do you think you .... ever live in another country?
3 .... you going to have a party to celebrate your birthday?
4 .... your parents let you stay by yourself in the house?
5 What .... you going to do when you get home?
6 .... you travel abroad for your next holiday?
7 What do you think you .... study when you leave school?
8 What time .... our next class?

5 Complete these sentences so that they are true for you. Then compare in pairs.

1 This weekend, I hope ....
2 Tomorrow, I'm going to ....
3 Next week, I'm having ....
4 Tonight, I'm going to watch ....
5 I'm sure I .... when I leave school.
6 I can't come to your house on Saturday because I ....

Reading

HEALTH

Reading Part 1

1 Match the sentences (1–10) with the correct meanings (a–d).

1 Students are required to wear trainers for sports activities.
2 Please throw all food rubbish in the green bin provided.
3 Warning: This water is unsafe to drink.
4 Each student is responsible for making sure the classroom is clean and tidy.
5 Students may bring a healthy snack to school.
6 It is forbidden to eat in the classroom.
7 Students aren't permitted to touch any cooking equipment.
8 Young people are advised to drink 500ml of milk per day.
9 It isn't necessary for students to bring a cake to school on their birthday.
10 Students are allowed to use mobile phones during the lunch hour.

a you can
b you can't
c you should/must
d you don't have to (but you can)

2 Where would you see the information in the sentences in Exercise 1? More than one answer may be possible.

A on a classroom noticeboard
B in an email to students/parents
C in a kitchen
D on a food label

> **Exam tip**
>
> When reading signs, labels and messages, it's important to understand who the information is for and why they may need it.

3 Choose the correct modal verb in each sign, label or message below. Then choose who each one is written for (a or b).

1 This sign is for people who want to
   a buy or pay for something.
   b know how to change some money.

> You *must / could* have the correct change for this machine.

2 This sign is for people who want to
   a take food away.
   b sit down in the café.

> Only customers who buy food at the café *may / could* eat here.

3 This information is for people who want to
   a know which ingredients to buy.
   b make something to eat.

> You *should / may* follow the cooking instructions.

4 This email is for
   a a friend.
   b a teacher.

> We *could / must* have a picnic, or if it isn't a nice day, what about going to Jack's Café for a burger?

» Page 87 **Modals (2)**

Reading

Reading Part 1

Exam task

For each question, choose the correct answer.

1

All students are invited to attend the school's 100th anniversary celebration. Please inform your teacher if you can provide any refreshments for the occasion.
Thank you
Mrs Long

A Students should tell their teacher if they can attend the celebration.
B Mrs Long is informing students that refreshments will be provided at the celebration.
C The school wants to know which students are able to bring food or drink to the celebration.

2

Heat soup in microwave for three minutes.
WARNING: may be very hot.

This label is advising people to
A make sure the soup is hot enough.
B avoid burning themselves.
C eat the soup cold if they wish.

3

SPECIAL OFFER
Free delivery service when you order three or more takeaway pizzas!

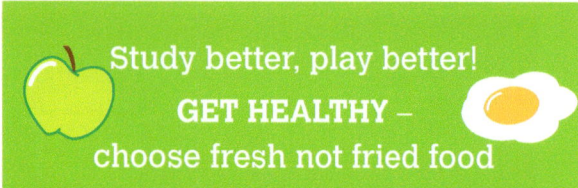

A Customers get a free pizza if they buy more than three.
B If you buy fewer than three pizzas, you have to pay for delivery.
C If you order a pizza from this company, it is delivered for free.

4

Study better, play better!
GET HEALTHY –
choose fresh not fried food

This notice is
A encouraging students to make healthy choices.
B warning students about the effects of a bad diet.
C forbidding students to eat fried food.

5

Eric
Can you send me your mum's recipe for chocolate cookies? It's Maya's birthday tomorrow and I want to bake some and bring them to school. I think she'd love them.
Thanks
Molly

Molly wants Eric to
A ask his mum to make some cookies for Maya.
B say if he thinks Maya would like some cookies for her birthday.
C email instructions for his mother's cookies.

Reading

Reading Part 6

1 Look at the photos and answer these questions. Then compare in pairs.

1. Which breakfast do you think is the healthiest?
2. Which one would you like to try? Why? / Why not?
3. What do you eat for breakfast on school days / at the weekend?
4. Do you think schools should provide healthy snacks for pupils? Why? / Why not?

2 Read the text in the exam task and answer these questions. Do not complete the gaps yet.

1. What problems are described?
2. Do you think there are similar problems in your country?

Exam task

For each question, write the correct answer. Write one word for each gap.

Breakfast

Everyone knows that it is very important to eat a good breakfast as part of a healthy diet. But about 20% of British school children say they sometimes don't have time to eat breakfast, while 7% say they hardly **(1)** .... eat breakfast before they leave home to go to school. This is a big problem because many pupils often eat unhealthy snacks instead **(2)** .... a proper breakfast and they are more likely to put **(3)** .... weight. They can also have trouble concentrating during lessons.

In the UK, **(4)** .... most popular things to eat for breakfast are cereal with milk, or toast with butter and jam. The traditional fried breakfast is something that people only eat occasionally or at the weekend. But many breakfast cereals contain too **(5)** .... sugar. This is bad for your teeth and also makes you feel hungry more quickly. In some countries, people eat things **(6)** .... as eggs, or fish with rice for breakfast, which people in other parts of the world eat for lunch or dinner.

3 Match the phrasal verbs with *put* (1–3) with the verbs with similar meanings (a–c).

1. He *put on* weight after he stopped running marathons.
2. 'It's very dark outside. I can't see anything.' 'I'll *put* my torch *on*.'
3. In Antarctica, you must *put* gloves and a hat *on* when you go outside.

a switch on
b increase
c wear

4 Choose the options which match the meaning of the phrasal verbs with *put*.

1. When you've finished, please can you *put away* the breakfast things.
   a put them on the table
   b put them in the cupboard
2. They *put* the fire *out* by throwing a blanket on it.
   a started
   b stopped
3. The café has *put up* its prices, so ice cream is more expensive.
   a increased
   b decreased
4. I've *put* my name *down* on the list for the next camping trip. I can't wait!
   a added
   b removed
5. They had to *put off* the race until the next day because of the storm.
   a cancel
   b delay

Exam tip

Prepositions are often tested in Reading Part 6. These can be prepositions of time (e.g. *on, before, after, since*), place (e.g. *at, in, on*) or prepositions which are part of phrasal verbs (e.g. *put on*).

UNIT 5　43

Speaking

Speaking Part 1
Pages 102–104

> **Exam tip**
> Be prepared to answer questions on both personal information and facts, using present, past and future forms.

1 🔊 22 Listen to Laura talking about her likes, dislikes and future plans.

Note down one thing that Laura …
1 likes eating.
2 hates eating.
3 is going to do this weekend.
4 is thinking of doing in the future.

2 Complete these phrases Laura uses.
1 I'm .... about cooking.
2 I'm always .... for some pasta when I get home from school.
3 I can't .... fish.
4 I'm really .... surfing.
5 There's .... I'll ever leave.

3 Put these words in the teacher's questions in the correct order.
1 favourite / What's / your / restaurant / ?
2 going / to / this / are / you / do / weekend / What / ?
3 about / something / the / plans / me / your / Tell / for / future / .
4 enjoy / after / doing / you / school / do / What / ?
5 like / you / cooking / Do / ?

4 Match these answers (A–E) with the questions in Exercise 3 (1–5).

A Oh, I haven't decided yet. I want to go to university, but I don't know what I want to study. I want to travel; to see London and maybe study there.

B I don't like making cakes. It makes too much mess and I hate doing the washing-up afterwards. But I often help my mum make dinner.

C It depends. If the weather's nice, I might go cycling with my dad. But if it isn't, I'll stay at home and play computer games.

D It's called Milo's. They have the best steak and chips there.

E I like to relax at home. I watch TV, I play the piano and I chat to my friends online.

> **Exam task**
>
> 🔊 23 Work in pairs. Listen to the examiner's questions and take turns to answer when your teacher pauses the recording.

> **Exam tip**
> Add more details to your answers. Don't just give one- or two-word answers.

Writing

Writing Part 1
Pages 95–97

1 👁 Exam candidates often make mistakes with modal verbs. Choose the correct verbs, then put the phrases into the correct category below. Can you add any more phrases?

1 If you don't fancy the beach, you *may / can* always go climbing and explore the lovely countryside around the mountains.
2 I thought that we *can / could* go and see *Dodge Ball*.
3 I am going to buy a DVD, but I don't know which … *should / could* you help me?
4 I think you *can / should* go to the countryside.

Suggesting	Requesting

📝 Page 87 **Modals (2)**

2 Read the email from Sam and the notes. Work in pairs. Think of some ideas to expand the notes.

Hi!
Mum says I can invite some friends for dinner on my birthday. I hope you can come. It will be next Thursday at 6 p.m. —— *Great!*
Do you think it's a good idea to have a barbecue in the garden? —— *Yes! Say why.*
Mum's going to make a cake and I want to make an apple pie, but I've never made one before, so I hope it will be OK! —— *Offer to help.*
After dinner, we could do some fun activities together. What do you think everyone would enjoy doing? —— *Suggest an activity …*
Bye for now
Sam

---

3 Read Frankie's answer to Sam's email. Compare your ideas with Frankie's, then correct the <u>six</u> grammar mistakes in the email.

Hi, Sam
That's great! Yes, I can come on Thursday. I can't wait! Yes, is a good idea having a barbecue for your birthday because it's summer and it's nice to be outside. It will be fun. I love cooking sausages. I can bring some for the barbecue or some drinks and snacks. Apple pie is my favourite dessert. I can come early to help you cook if you will like. My grandma taught me how to make it. After dinner, I think we should play some games and then watch the movie. Why don't watch the new Star Wars movie? We need to choose something that everyone love and it's one of the best film.
See you on Saturday.
Frankie

✅ Exam task

Read this email from your new friend Mateo, who has recently moved to your city, and the notes you have made.

Write your email to Mateo using all the notes.

Write about 100 words.

💡 Exam tip
Make sure you give reasons for your suggestions.

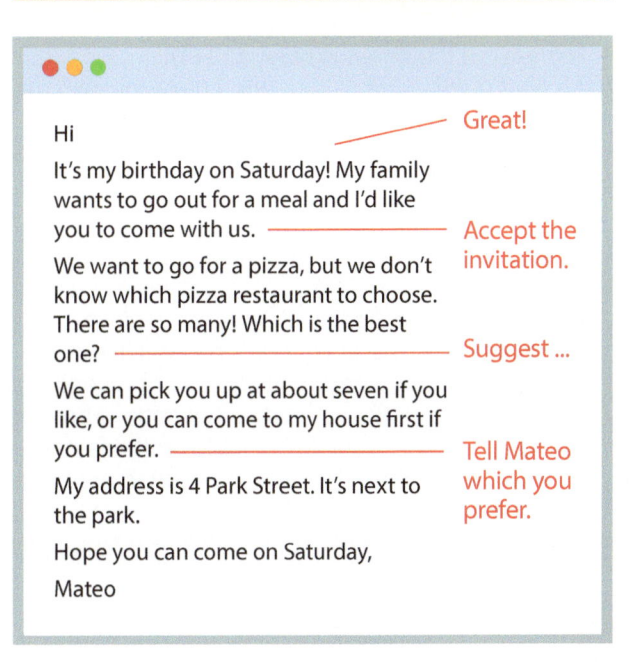

Hi
It's my birthday on Saturday! My family wants to go out for a meal and I'd like you to come with us. —— *Great! / Accept the invitation.*
We want to go for a pizza, but we don't know which pizza restaurant to choose. There are so many! Which is the best one? —— *Suggest …*
We can pick you up at about seven if you like, or you can come to my house first if you prefer. —— *Tell Mateo which you prefer.*
My address is 4 Park Street. It's next to the park.
Hope you can come on Saturday,
Mateo

UNIT 5

6 My home

Reading

Reading Part 3

1 Look at these photos of two very different homes. Which one would you prefer to live in? Why?

2 Work in pairs. Look at the words and phrases in the box. Choose a word and tell your partner the meaning. Do not say the word.

> balcony   coast   comfortable   convenient   cosy   countryside
> crowded   cultural events   freezing   historical buildings
> huge   lively   peaceful   space   traditional   view

This word means when the weather is very cold – the temperature is below zero.

Freezing?

3 Choose words from Exercise 2 to complete this text about a girl called Léa and where she lives. Then compare in pairs.

My home by Léa Dupont

I live with my parents and twin brother in a small town near our capital city. We're in the north of the country, so it can be **(1)** .... in the winter, but the summers are warm. There are trains that run from my town straight to the capital, so it's quite **(2)** .... to get there. We can also drive to the **(3)** .... if we want to spend time at the beach, although it's a long journey.

Our house is in a narrow street, which I think makes the house a bit too dark inside. But it also means there aren't many cars driving past, which is great, as the street is quiet and **(4)** .... Our house has quite a lot of **(5)** .... and I have my own room. It's the smallest room in the house, but it feels really **(6)** .... My parents are very sociable people, so the house is always full of visitors, and life is rarely dull!

The capital is a big, **(7)** .... city with lots to do. My parents love all the cultural events like exhibitions, and I love shopping in the department stores. They're **(8)** .... – much bigger than the shops in my town – but also much more expensive, so I can't really afford to buy anything there. My grandparents live in the heart of the city, in one of the luxury apartments that were recently built there. They have a lovely big **(9)** .... outside, where you get an amazing **(10)** .... of the city. My brother's not a city person, though – when we're there, he's always keen to get home again as quickly as possible!

4 🔊 24 Listen and check.

Exam tip

If you're not sure which option to choose, cross out the ones you know are definitely wrong. Remember, your answers **must** come from the text, not your own opinion.

5 Look at these questions about Léa. Choose the correct answer (A, B or C) based on the text. Underline the phrase from the text that shows the correct answer. Then compare your answers in pairs.

1 What does Léa say about her town?
   A It never gets very cold during the year.
   B It's at the seaside.
   C It's close to the capital city.

2 How does Léa feel about the house she lives in?
   A She would like more space in her room.
   B She has mixed feelings about its location.
   C She thinks it's sometimes too crowded.

3 Léa says that the capital city has
   A some smart new flats in the centre.
   B something for all of her family to enjoy.
   C big stores where she buys clothes.

6 Work in pairs. Take turns to talk about where you live. Talk about your town or city, and the kind of home you live in.

HOUSE & HOME

Reading

Exam task

For each question, choose the correct answer.

THIS IS WHAT IT'S LIKE TO LIVE IN A TREE HOUSE

Luke Jackson and his parents moved from their apartment in Vancouver, Canada, to a tree house in the forest.

Earlier this year, I moved into a tree house. It had been my family's dream ever since we read an article on a website about people who live in unusual homes. My parents decided to design our new home without the help of an architect, so they spent hours watching online videos and reading library books to get ideas for our tree house. Now that we've finished it, it's exactly how we wanted to have it.

Our tree house is built around a very strong tree, so it can support the two floors that surround it. I used to have a big bedroom in our old apartment, but now my room is pretty small. However, I don't mind that at all because now it has an incredible view of the forest in every direction. It's fantastic – I really couldn't imagine living anywhere else now. Our next project is to finish the garden – it's going to be amazing one day.

I'll never forget the first night we spent in the tree house. When I was in bed, I started to notice how the tree house actually felt. I hadn't expected it to move in the wind like a boat on the ocean. However, it was quite relaxing and didn't take long to get used to. It was also really dark, because there are no street lights!

We don't have any neighbours nearby, so I spend a lot of time on my own painting and playing music in my room. What's great is that I can make a noise when I play my guitar up there since I live in the middle of the forest! I only wish more of my paintings could fit on my wall, instead of being in a big pile on the floor! My friend's coming to stay next weekend and I can't wait to welcome him to my home! I've already warned him that it'll be a bit crowded in my room, but that won't stop us from having fun together!

1. Where did Luke's family get the idea to build a tree house from?
   A from talking to another family member
   B from the internet and library books
   C from an architect
   D from an unusual home they visited

2. What does Luke like most about the design of the tree house?
   A what he can see from his room
   B its position in the garden
   C the size of his room
   D the tree it's built around

3. On his first night in the tree house, Luke was …
   A surprised by the way it moved.
   B afraid of the noises he heard.
   C relaxed because it was so dark.
   D worried because there were no lights.

4. What else does Luke say about his bedroom now?
   A It is too close to his nearest neighbours.
   B It is a good place to play a musical instrument.
   C It has enough wall space for all his paintings.
   D It has plenty of room when friends come and visit him.

5. What might Luke write in a blog about his family's tree house?

   A | My family wasn't sure if we would be able to live in a tree house until we found an architect who could help us.

   B | I love living somewhere where all my friends can come and hang out in my room.

   C | Even though we haven't started looking after our garden, I prefer spending time there because it's just wild flowers and lots of trees.

   D | Moving from an apartment to a tree house has been an exciting adventure – it's a very different type of home.

UNIT 6

Grammar

used to
>> Page 87

1 Read this explanation of *used to*.

On page 47, Luke describes his bedroom like this:

*I **used to have** a big bedroom in our old apartment.*

We use *used to* to talk about things in the past that are no longer true. His bedroom was big before, but now it isn't.

Now complete these sentences with the correct form of *used to*.

1 My mum .... take me to the park every day when I was small.
2 .... (you) play computer games when you were younger?
3 I .... go out in the evenings, but I go out a lot now.
4 My older sister .... play with me very much when I was a child. She said I was too annoying.
5 .... (she) have long hair when she was ten?
6 I .... ride my bike to school every day, but now I go on the bus.

Verbs followed by infinitive / -ing form
>> Page 88

2 Look at these sentences from the text on page 47:

*It's exactly how we **wanted to have** it.*
*I really couldn't **imagine living** anywhere else now.*

Complete this table with 'infinitive' or '-ing form'.

Verbs followed by (1)	Verbs followed by (2) ....
apologise for	advise
avoid	agree
consist of	forget
imagine	intend
look forward to	learn
suggest	offer
	persuade
	plan
	promise
	teach
	want

3 Correct the mistakes in these sentences written by exam candidates.

1 Don't forget go to the shops and buy milk.
2 I would enjoy to see a show, especially a fashion show.
3 The bookshop needs people working for up to six months.
4 We should consider to make tourist programmes.

4 Complete these sentences with the correct form of the verbs in brackets.

1 My older sister wants to learn .... (drive) as soon as possible.
2 I can't imagine .... (lose) my mobile. My parents would be very angry!
3 I had to apologise to my mum for .... (break) her favourite vase.
4 My dad offered .... (take) me to my friend's house in the car.
5 Jay suggested .... (go) to the cinema, but I didn't have any money.
6 I didn't really want to go out tonight, but my friend persuaded me .... (go).

do, make, have, go
>> Page 89

5 Look at what Luke says about his guitar on page 47.

*I can **make a noise** when I play my guitar up there.*

Correct the mistakes in these sentences written by exam candidates. Which verb should replace the underlined verb?

1 I'm going to <u>do</u> a lot of sandwiches and salads for the picnic.
2 We have decided to <u>make</u> a sports day.
3 Next week, we want to <u>make</u> a party.
4 I have to <u>do</u> shopping today in the big shopping centre.
5 I am going to climb mountains and <u>do</u> fishing.
6 Next week, we are going to <u>do</u> a volleyball match at the club.
7 They also had rooms to sit down in and <u>make</u> your homework.

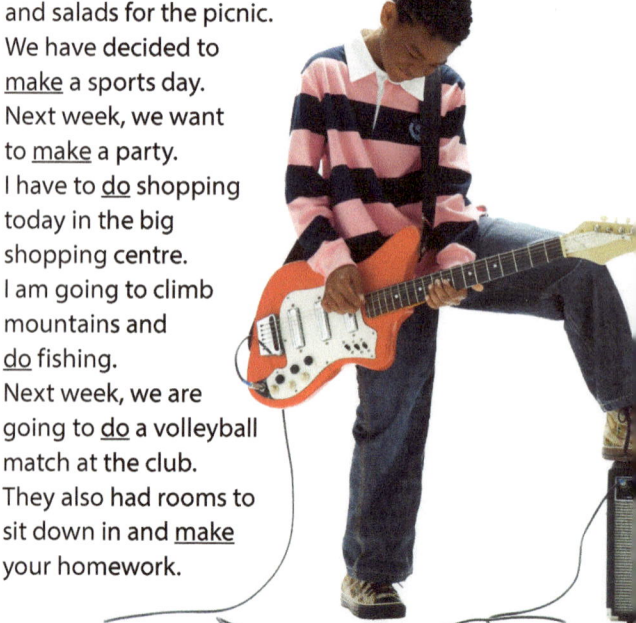

48

Reading

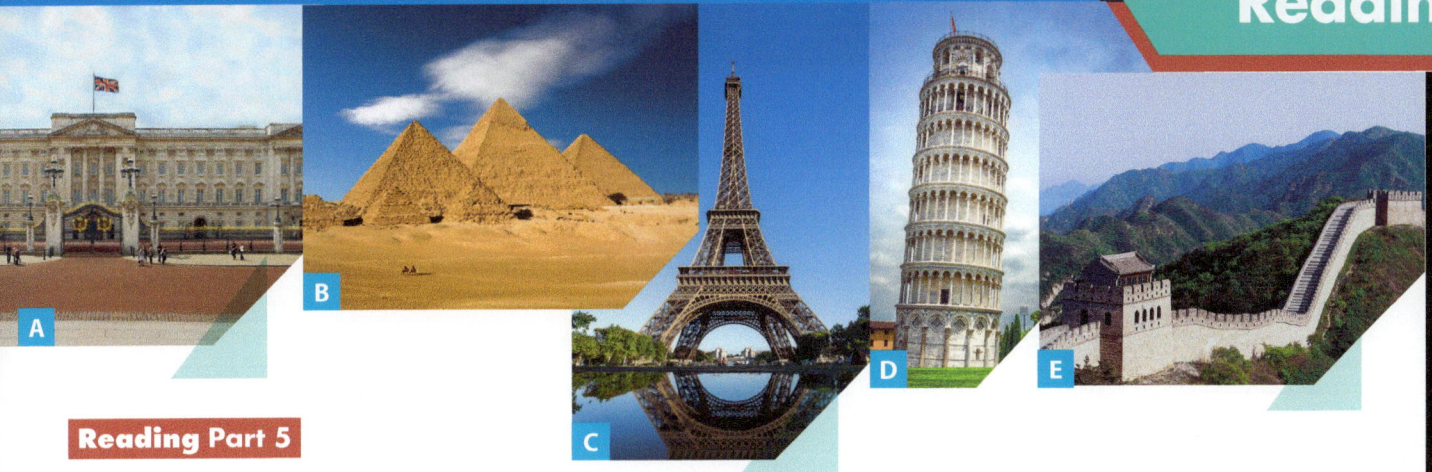

PLACES & BUILDINGS

Reading Part 5

1 Work in pairs. Which famous buildings and places do you know around the world? Look at the photos above to help you.

2 Match the names with the photos (A–E).

Buckingham Palace   the Eiffel Tower   the Great Wall of China
the Leaning Tower of Pisa   the Pyramids

Exam tip
Try writing a word in the gap before you look at the options. This can help you when you come to make your choices.

Exam task

For each question, choose the correct answer.

THE TAJ MAHAL

What's the most beautiful building you've ever visited? Many people (1) .... that the Taj Mahal, built in India in the 17th century, is one of the most magnificent buildings they've ever seen. For example, its walls are made of white marble, which almost seems to change colour depending on the (2) .... of light shining on it. What's more, in some of the gardens that (3) .... the building, there are wonderful fountains and pools of water.

Nowadays, the Taj Mahal (4) .... up to 8 million visitors every year, coming from all over the world. However, increasing (5) .... of pollution in the environment, from vehicles in the area, are becoming a serious (6) .... for the building, so people are no longer permitted to drive close to it. Visitors must either walk from the parking areas or catch a special bus.

1	A	advise	B	decide	C	suppose	D	agree
2	A	amount	B	total	C	sum	D	whole
3	A	support	B	consist	C	involve	D	surround
4	A	introduces	B	finds	C	attracts	D	produces
5	A	heights	B	types	C	levels	D	loads
6	A	trouble	B	issue	C	doubt	D	event

3 Work in pairs. Discuss these questions.

1 What can you remember about the Taj Mahal from the text?

2 Have you ever been to any of the places in the photos above? Which one would you most like to visit? Why?

UNIT 6   49

Writing

Writing Part 2
Pages 100–101

Exam tip

For the story option in Writing Part 2, you'll be given a sentence to begin your story. Before you start, make a brief plan to organise your ideas.

1 Work in pairs. Look at the places in the box. Which ones would you like to go to? Why? What could you do there? Who would you go with?

> a beach   a castle   a city   a desert   a forest
> an island   a jungle   a lake   a mountain
> an old house   a village

2 Work in pairs. Choose one of the places in the box in Exercise 1 and write down some ideas for a story about the place you have chosen. Think about these things:

- Who is in the story?
- Why did they go there?
- What happened?
- How does the story end?

Linking words

Exam tip

When you write in English, think about how to join your ideas together.

3 Read Holly's story about a city she visited. Her teacher asked her to begin her story with this sentence:

My parents organised a big surprise for my birthday last Saturday.

> My parents organised a big surprise for my birthday last Saturday. It was a day trip to London – and it was fantastic!
>
> When we <u>first</u> arrived, we set off to explore the city, <u>despite</u> the rain! We walked all the way along the river <u>and</u> spent the morning at Tate Modern, a huge art gallery. We also had a ride on the London Eye <u>because</u> we wanted to see right across the city – and we weren't disappointed! <u>Although</u> it was cloudy, we still saw some wonderful views, <u>so</u> we were really pleased. <u>In the evening</u>, we took a bus tour around different parts of the city, which was great fun, then we ate in a really nice restaurant. <u>After that</u>, we went home. We were tired but very happy. It was the best birthday I've ever had!

Match the underlined words in the story with the categories in this table.

Time links	
Links to explain reason	
Links to explain result	
Links to add a point	
Links to contrast a point	

4 Now read this story about a day at a museum. Complete it with linking words from Exercise 3. Use the words in brackets to help you.

The student had to begin the story with this sentence:

Samuel's mum decided to take him to the museum for the day.

> Samuel's mum decided to take him to the museum for the day. When they arrived at the museum, it was still quite early in the morning, **(1)** .... (result) they decided to go to the café for some breakfast, which was delicious.
>
> **(2)** .... (contrast) the museum had just opened, there were quite a few people in there. Then Samuel and his mum set off around the museum. **(3)** .... (time link), they went to look at the Egyptian section and **(4)** .... (time link) they went inside a special room **(5)** .... (reason) Samuel wanted to see the beautiful old paintings in there. **(6)** .... (contrast) it was quite crowded, they managed to see everything **(7)** .... (add a point) they were even allowed to take pictures, **(8)** .... (result) that was great! They spent the whole day at the museum. It was quite expensive, **(9)** .... (contrast) they didn't mind **(10)** .... (reason) they'd had a good time!

Writing

5 ⊙ Exam candidates sometimes make mistakes with punctuation and linking words. Correct the mistakes in these sentences.

1. I was a little bit worried, what it would be like.
   I was a little bit worried about what it would be like.
2. I want to inform you, we're going to the Odeon cinema.
3. The bride and groom's family will invite their friends, relatives to the ceremony.
4. I am not coming to the class tomorrow. I can't come, I'm going to the dentist.
5. Centre Park is beautiful and there are a lot of animals, which you can feed because they are very friendly.

> **Exam tip**
> When you're writing sentences, it's important to think about where one sentence ends and the next one begins.

6 Look at this story written by a boy called Alex, about his trip to the beach. His story had to begin with this sentence:

We put everything into the car and set off early in the morning.

Decide where each sentence ends and add appropriate punctuation. Then compare in pairs.

we put everything into the car and set off early in the morning the sun was shining and it was hot we had brought a picnic with us to eat on the beach we were quite hungry so we were really looking forward to it finally we arrived at the beach the sea was really blue and it was a beautiful day we got everything out of the car and raced down to the sea my brother and I got changed and went swimming immediately then we ate the picnic it was delicious we spent the whole day on the beach and then came home as the sun was going down and just as it began to get cold it was a great day

7 🔊 25 Listen to Alex talking about his day at the beach and check your answers. Can you split the answer into three paragraphs?

> **Exam task**
>
> Your English teacher has asked you to write a story. Your story must begin with this sentence:
>
> *Jack and his dad took their backpacks and started walking towards the mountain.*
>
> Write your **story** in about **100 words**.

> **Exam tip**
> Write down a few ideas before you start writing so that you know you have enough to say. Don't forget to write only about 100 words.

UNIT 6 51

Listening

Listening Part 1

✓ Exam task

🔊 26 For each question, choose the correct answer.

1 What does the girl like about her town?

A   B   C

2 What would the girl like to buy?

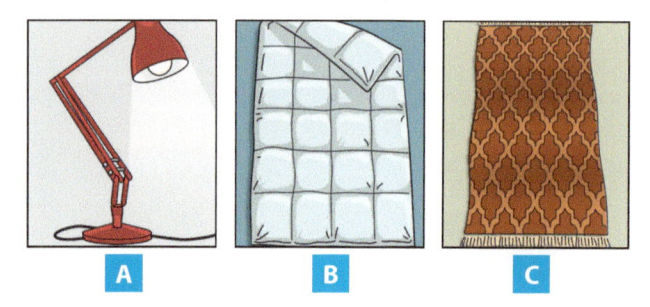

A   B   C

3 What will the weather be like at the weekend?

A   B   C

4 What did the boy dislike about the hotel room he stayed in?

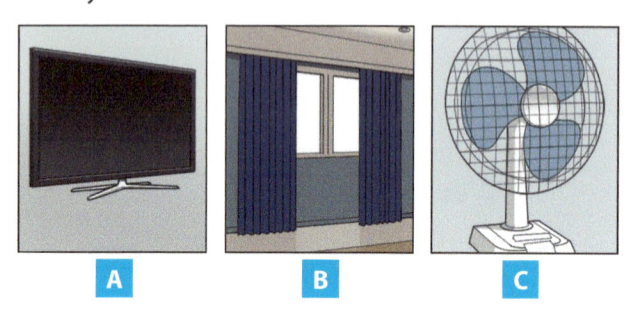

A   B   C

💡 Exam tip

Before each dialogue starts, look carefully at the question and the pictures to make sure you understand exactly what you're listening for.

5 Who came to talk to the girl's class at school?

A   B   C

6 Which drink did the boy and girl have during their school trip?

A   B   C

7 Which birthday present will the girl buy for her sister?

A   B   C

52

Speaking

Speaking Part 3
>> Pages 110–111

1 Put these phrases into the correct category in the table below.

> What do you think?   I think … would be more useful for them.   How/What about taking … ?
> I think they should take … rather than …   They'd probably take …   That's a good idea, isn't it?

Giving opinions	Making suggestions	Asking for opinions

2 🔊 **27** Listen to Saskia and Oscar talking about a trip to a city. Complete their conversation with phrases from Exercise 1.

Saskia: What do you think they should take with them on the trip, Oscar?
Oscar: I think it would be useful to take a guidebook.
Saskia: That's **(1)** .... ? And **(2)** .... an umbrella?
Oscar: I think a coat **(3)** .... It could be cold and windy!
Saskia: OK, well, **(4)** .... an umbrella **(5)** .... a coat.
Oscar: Fine.

✓ Exam task

🔊 **28** Listen to the examiner and do the task.

> 💡 **Exam tip**
> There's no 'correct' answer to this part of the exam. The important thing is the language you use to discuss the options.

UNIT 6

7 In the wild

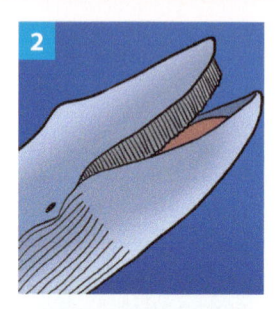

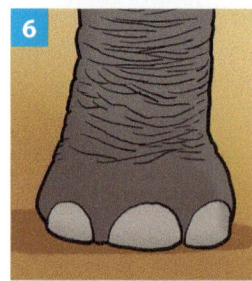

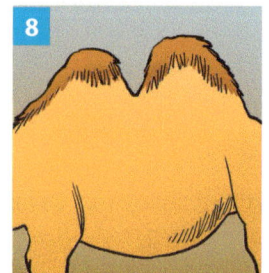

THE NATURAL WORLD

Vocabulary

1 Match the pictures (1–10) with the words in the box.

> bat   camel   elephant   gorilla   parrot
> penguin   shark   snake   spider   whale

2 Answer these questions about the creatures in Exercise 1.

Which creatures ...
1 have fur?
2 have wings?
3 are vegetarian?
4 hunt other creatures?
5 have a very good sense of smell?

3 Can you name any more species of insect/bird/fish?

4 Complete the statements below with the words in the box.

> cruel   protect   rare   wildlife

1 People aren't doing enough to .... animals like tigers and elephants.
2 Many people think it's .... to keep wild animals in cages.
3 One of the best places to see a variety of .... is in Kenya or South Africa.
4 Zoos are a safe environment for animals that are becoming .... in the wild.

5 Read these notices and answer the questions.

A IT IS FORBIDDEN TO FEED THE ANIMALS.

B Sorry, the giraffe house is CLOSED for cleaning. ONLY STAFF MAY ENTER.

C Please use the recycling bins provided.

D Talk starts at 3.30. 'LIONS IN DANGER' All ages welcome.

E Never leave food in your tent – bears may try to take it.

1 Which of the notices A–E would you *not* see at a zoo?
2 Which of the notices is/are:
  a telling you not to do something?
  b inviting you to do something?
  c making a request?
  d warning you about a danger?
  e telling you when you can do something?

6 When was the last time you visited a zoo or safari park? What did you like / not like about it?

Listening

Listening Part 4

1 🔊 29 You will hear an interview with a man called Martin, who works in a zoo. Look at question 1 in the exam task below, listen to the first part of the recording and answer these questions.

1 Are all the animals in question 1 mentioned?
2 Who says the word *popular*, Martin or the interviewer?
3 What information do you hear which shows the animals are popular?

2 Before you listen to the whole interview, underline the key words in questions 2–6 and the options.

✓ Exam task

🔊 30 For each question, choose the correct answer.

1 What are the most popular animals at the zoo?
   A the penguins
   B the lions
   C the monkeys

2 How has the zoo changed in the last 25 years?
   A There is a wider range of animals.
   B The animals have more space.
   C More of the animals have babies.

3 What's the most difficult part of his job?
   A being in dangerous situations
   B getting up early
   C spending so much time cleaning

4 To stop the animals from getting bored, the zookeepers
   A change the animals' diet.
   B play games with them.
   C change where they put the animals' food.

5 Martin mainly works with gorillas because they
   A need an experienced person to look after them.
   B like to have regular contact with the same people.
   C are his favourite animals.

6 Martin was surprised that gorillas are so
   A frightening.
   B peaceful.
   C sociable.

💡 Exam tip
The words you hear may not be exactly the same as the words in the options, so listen for words which have a similar meaning.

3 Look at these adjectives from the exam task. Think of other ways to say the same thing.

1 difficult   *something that is hard to do*
2 dangerous
3 bored
4 experienced
5 favourite
6 happy
7 peaceful
8 generous

4 👁 Exam candidates sometimes make mistakes with the spelling of adjectives. Correct the mistakes in these sentences.

1 I know you don't like it here, but I think it's a beatiful town.
2 The room was very warm and confortable.
3 All of my friends are from diffrent countries.
4 My new teacher is exellent.
5 I found this awsome game online.
6 They filmed a tipical day in class that will be shown on TV.

UNIT 7

Grammar

Past perfect
Page 89

1 Look at these examples of the past perfect. Choose the correct words to complete the statements below.

*The zoo **had already moved** the bigger animals to give them more space when Martin started working there 25 years ago.*

*Martin **hadn't realised** the gorillas were so gentle until he started working with them.*

1 The zoo moved the bigger animals *before / after* Martin started working there.
2 Martin realised that gorillas were gentle *before / after* he started working with them.

The zoo moved the bigger animals. | Martin started working there.

Martin started working with gorillas. | He realised they were gentle.

2 Complete this rule.

The past perfect is formed with the past simple form of the verb .... and the ....

3 Listen to a news report. Are these sentences true (T) or false (F)?

1 The zookeeper found the tiger.
2 The tiger escaped out of the zoo into the town.
3 No one was hurt.
4 The tiger escaped after breakfast.

4 Listen again and choose the correct options to complete these sentences.

1 A visitor *had / hadn't* phoned the police to say the tiger was missing.
2 The tiger *had / hadn't* escaped before.
3 The zookeeper *had / hadn't* forgotten to lock the cage door.
4 The zookeeper said the tiger *had / hadn't* been hungry.

5 Complete these sentences with the past simple or past perfect of the verbs in brackets.

1 The zookeeper .... (discover) the tiger .... (escape) at lunchtime.
2 We .... (cannot) go home until my little brother .... (see) every animal at the zoo.
3 It .... (be) the first time the baby tiger .... (appear) at the zoo.
4 Before I .... (come) to this school, I .... (not study) English.
5 I .... (never see) a snake in the wild until I .... (visit) Australia.
6 We .... (go) to my grandparents' house last month, but before that I .... (not be) there for nearly a year.

6 Look at these pictures. What had Super Sam done by the ages of 5, 10 and 12?

By the age of five, Super Sam had learned to drive a car.

5 learn / drive
10 sail / round world
12 leave / university

7 Work in pairs. Discuss these questions.

1 What do you think happened to the zookeeper and to the tiger in the story?
2 Have any of your pets ever escaped? What happened?
3 What had/hadn't you done by the ages of 5/10/12?

Reading

Reading Part 6

1 Write the missing words.

1. **I'm having a great time in Antarctica.**
   She said she .... having a great time in Antarctica.

2. **I had a great time in Antarctica.**
   She said she had .... a great time in Antarctica.

3. **I will have a great time in Antarctica.**
   She said she .... have a great time in Antarctica.

4. **Have you had a great time in Antarctica?**
   She asked me .... I'd had a great time in Antarctica.

5. **Have a great time in Antarctica!**
   She told me .... have a great time in Antarctica.

6. **Don't go to Antarctica!**
   She told me .... to go to Antarctica.

📝 » Page 90 **Reported speech**

2 Complete the sentences below with the words in the box.

> it   not   to   whether

1. My mum told me .... to get lost in the snow!
2. The doctor said .... was important to eat a lot of chocolate while camping in Antarctica.
3. Yesterday, someone asked .... I wanted to go whale watching.
4. It smelled horrible, but my friend persuaded me .... try seal meat.

✅ **Exam task**

💡 Exam tip
Reading Part 6 often tests auxiliary verbs, e.g. *do/did/does* in question forms, *have* in the present and past perfect, and *be* in the present and past continuous.

For each question, write the correct answer. Write one word for each gap.

LIVING IN ANTARCTICA

I've always wanted to go to Antarctica because my dad spent several months every year working there as a scientist before I was born. He said it was the quietest and most beautiful place he (1) .... ever been to.
So when I got a job at one of the research stations, I was really excited. All my friends thought I was mad and tried to persuade me (2) .... to go. They couldn't understand why I wanted to live (3) .... that was so cold and far (4) .... home. But I love it. In the summer, we spend our weekends kayaking, fishing and climbing volcanoes. In the winter, it can get boring (5) .... it's dark 24 hours a day. But it's more fun (6) .... I expected because all the staff watch lots of movies and play games together. On 21 June, we celebrate mid-winter with a big party.

3 Work in pairs. Think of three reasons why you would / would not like to live in Antarctica.

UNIT 7

Reading

Reading Part 2

1 Is litter a problem at your school or in your town? How do you think people can solve this problem?

2 Complete the worries below with the words/phrases in the box.

climate change   litter   oil   pollution

1 I'm worried about .... on the streets. It's a huge problem in my city. People just throw rubbish out of their car windows.

2 I'm extremely worried about .... I think sea levels will rise and there will be lots of big floods.

3 I'm worried about what will happen when we run out of .... I don't think anyone has found a solution to this problem yet.

4 I'm really worried about .... in the local river. There are hardly any fish in it now.

3 Which of the issues in Exercise 2 are you most worried about? Why?

Exam task

For each question, choose the correct answer.

The teenagers below all want to work as volunteers to help the environment.

On the opposite page there are descriptions of eight clubs which help the environment.

Decide which club would be the most suitable for the people below.

Exam tip

Underline three things that are important for each person. Make sure the option you choose matches *everything* they require.

1 Ali lives in the country and wants to help wildlife in his area. He has experience caring for animals and would like to share this knowledge with other young people.

2 Sam lives in a harbour town and is worried about the amount of pollution in his area. He wants to know what effect this is having on the local wildlife and he would also like to take part in events to help reduce pollution where he lives.

3 Hannah only has free time at the weekend and wants to meet other teenagers interested in making things out of materials that are recycled. She wants to help organise a social event to make more people in her town start reducing the amount of rubbish they throw away.

4 Fatema has brilliant computer skills and would love to join a club that meets online. She wants to share information to let people know which animals are in danger and ways to help them.

5 Joe lives in a city and wants to meet other people who are interested in the environment. He wants to know how pollution affects plants and learn how to grow food in a city garden project.

Clubs working to help the environment

A Safe Zone
We provide a safe place for wildlife such as bats, snakes and rabbits that have been injured. Our team of experts care for them until they're healthy enough to go back into nature. Our team wants to train more young people to help us with jobs like cleaning the cages and preparing the animals' food.

B Earth's Friends
We get creative at Earth's Friends! This youth club is for teens who want to get involved with online projects such as making more people aware of pollution in cities and how it is affecting the climate. Our website has a fantastic travel planner, so you can see how walking or cycling reduces pollution in your local area.

C Eco-Teen
Come and help clean up rubbish in our city parks! It's not easy, but you'll make loads of new friends who share the same passion as you do. And it's not all hard work – we have summer barbecues, guest speakers and group discussions about how we can help to protect animals in the area.

D Green Time
Come and learn about all the different species that live in our local fields, woods and back gardens. And if you've got any experience looking after animals, let us know! We're short on youth volunteers who can offer tips and advice at our weekly teen meetings in villages and towns across the nation. Our club wants to provide a safer environment for local creatures – big and small – by holding talks and events.

E Listen Up!
You can access our weekly meetings from any time zone on our award-winning website, where you can chat with young people concerned about the environment. Our members are passionate about making people aware of the things everyone should do to save and protect species all over the Earth. Members post updates and articles about wildlife issues weekly.

F Genius!
Don't put your bottles, newspapers and tin cans in the recycling bin – bring them to any Saturday-morning meeting, when our expert environmental artist shows you how to make art out of rubbish! Take part in planning the annual event to show off your creative projects to the public, and share tips on ways to reduce waste.

G Nature First
Come and get some fresh air and meet people of all ages concerned about the environment at our beach project, where we collect plastic to be recycled in a coastal area near you. Learn how waste in our oceans harms sea life and what you can do about it.

H Band Together
You won't believe you're in the middle of the city where our club meets every Sunday afternoon. Come and see all of the different crops we produce at our little farm. Young and old are invited to come and find out when to pick what you've planted when you join Band Together. We also discuss monthly topics such as vehicles and how they affect nature.

4 What can you do to help the environment in your area?

Speaking

Speaking Part 2
Pages 105–109

1. Tick (✓) the things you can see in the photos below.

   desert   ice   jungle   ocean   river
   sunset   waterfall

2. Which of these adjectives can you use to describe the things below (1–3)?

   calm   clear   freezing   frozen   humid

   1 the weather
   2 the sky
   3 the sea / a river

3. Complete the sentences below with the words in the box.

   like   must   probably   sure

   1 I think it .... be winter.
   2 It looks .... it's going to rain.
   3 I think the people are .... scientists.
   4 I'm not ...., but I think this might be in Thailand.

Exam tip

It's a good idea to start by talking about the location and season or time of day. You should use the passive for this, e.g. *I think this photo was taken in winter because the people are wearing warm clothes.*

Page 92   **The passive: present & past**

4. Choose the correct options to complete these sentences.

   1 The boat *is left / was left* in the ice because they couldn't get it out.
   2 Their clothes *were probably made / are probably made* of wool – they look really warm.
   3 The animals *take / are taken* to the river every day.
   4 The birds *fed / were fed* with special food.

Exam task

Work in pairs.

Student A: Describe photo 1.

Student B: Describe photo 2.

Try to include as many details as you can about …

- the people: what they are doing / what they are wearing / what they look like / how you think they are feeling
- the place: what the weather is like / where you think it is / what time of year/day the photo was taken.

5. 🔊 32 Listen to two students describing the photos. Note down the words and phrases they use from this unit.

Writing

Writing Part 2
Pages 98–99

1 Look at these photos and think of words to describe the weather.

A

B

2 Read this exam task. Match the underlined words/phrases in the student's article on the right with the teacher's comments below it (1–4).

> You see this announcement in a nature magazine.
>
> **Articles wanted!**
> **A DAY IN THE COUNTRYSIDE**
>
> Can you remember a day you spent in the countryside? Where did you spend it? What did you do there? What did you like about this particular day? Tell us about it!
>
> Write an article answering these questions and we will publish the most interesting articles in our magazine.
>
> Write your **article** in about **100 words**.

3 Use the teacher's comments to rewrite the article.

Exam task

> You see this announcement in a magazine.
>
> **Articles wanted!**
> **YOUR FAVOURITE SEASON**
>
> Which is your favourite season? Why do you like this particular season? What is the weather like during this season? What special things do you do at this time of year? Tell us about it!
>
> Write an article answering these questions and we will publish the most interesting articles in our magazine.
>
> Write your **article** in about **100 words**.

We went to a lot of <u>nice</u> places in Ireland, but my favourite day was when we rented bicycles. We cycled on a path <u>which</u> used to be a railway. Now it's just for bikes and people walking, not cars. The weather was very good. We saw lots of birds and flowers and mountains. We had a picnic. We cycled 30km. A bus <u>picked us up</u>. We <u>didn't have to</u> cycle back again.

General comment: Some of this is very good, but try to add some more details to make it more interesting. Some of the sentences are too short and you've only written 73 words.

1 Can you think of a more interesting adjective?
2 Great to use this structure here!
3 Great to use a phrasal verb!
4 Great to use a relative pronoun!

Exam tip
Try to use some more advanced structures in your article (e.g. *used to*, phrasal verbs, passives). This will help you get a better mark.

4 Check your article. Have you included some of the following?

- a range of tenses (past, present, future)
- *used to*
- a comparative form
- a phrasal verb
- adjectives
- linking words
- a relative pronoun

UNIT 7 61

8 We're off!

Reading

Reading Part 3

1 Work in pairs. Discuss these questions.

1. What's your favourite way of travelling? By car, bus, plane, train or ship? Why?
2. Look at the photos. Which of these ways of travelling would you like to try? Which ones wouldn't you like to try? Why not?

2 Look at the words and phrases in the box. Are they used to talk about travelling by car, plane, train or ship? Put them into the correct category. Which words could go in more than one category?

| airport   boarding pass   check in   crowded   gate |
| harbour   land   motorway   pilot   platform |
| rough   roundabout   seat belt   security   station |
| take off   traffic jam   traffic lights   waves   weigh |

Car	Plane

Train	Ship

3 Use words and phrases from Exercise 2 to complete these sentences.

1. When we got to the check-in desk, we had to .... our luggage to see how heavy it was.
2. The .... was full of boats offering trips around the bay.
3. Don't forget to fasten your .... before we drive off.
4. Which .... does the train to Manchester go from?
5. We haven't moved for over ten minutes. This is a terrible ....!
6. Passengers for the flight to Paris should go to .... number 24.
7. If the sea is .... when you're on a ship, you may feel unwell.
8. You can drive faster on a .... than on other roads.

4 Read what three teenagers say about different journeys they have made. How were they travelling: by plane, ship or car?

Molly: We knew when we all got in that we had a long journey ahead. We looked at the map to see which places we'd pass through, so that we could help Dad find the way.

Samir: I had a lot of stuff to take with me, but luckily it wasn't too heavy. After we'd taken off, I had a snack and a drink and I watched a really funny film.

Jude: I thought the bad weather would make the journey unpleasant, so I took a tablet and I was fine. I just sat and watched the big waves outside the window.

5 Look at this question. Choose the correct answer: A, B, C or D.

What does Molly say about her trip?

A Her father knew how to get to where they were going.
B They were travelling to somewhere that was far away.
C She wasn't sure what their final destination was.
D They had planned the route together before the journey.

Reading

Exam task

For each question, choose the correct answer.

Exam tip

Underline the part of the text where you find the answer.

VISITING LONDON

I'm Marcus, and I live in Australia with my family. However, recently I flew to London with my parents for a holiday – the first time I'd been on a plane! We visited all the sights, especially my mum's favourites, as she'd lived in London with my grandparents, before they all moved to Australia.

For me, though, the most interesting was Tower Bridge, which I'd seen in photos of London. It had been my ambition to walk across it since I was young, so my parents were keen to take me, and Dad suddenly decided he wanted to see the new walkways between the two towers, 42 metres above the river. Some of the floor is made of thick glass so visitors can look down onto the bridge and the pavements for walkers either side, and then the river below.

The website says that, just as on a similar bridge in China, the glass is impossible to break, but I still imagined the walkways to be scary and I started wondering about walking across. What would happen if I didn't manage it? Even a friend who loves heights admitted he'd found it slightly worrying! Despite that, I didn't pay attention to what he said and decided to go anyway.

Once we arrived, my parents decided to stay at ground level, so I went over the walkways by myself. It was amazing! I'd read that the planners had aimed to make these areas look like big holes in the floor, and they certainly achieved that. In fact, the effect was so convincing that many visitors seemed nervous and avoided stepping on the glass sections, which was very amusing. After I returned to the ground, we saw the exhibition about the bridge's engineers, and how they keep it all working.

The bridge opens over 800 times a year, to allow large boats to pass underneath. By pure luck, we were standing by the bridge when a cruise ship passed through – amazing! In fact, it was so enormous, I was much less interested in the bridge for a moment! Then I realised that for a great view of it, you probably need to be on board a ship. Somehow, I don't think our next holiday will be a cruise to London, though!

1 Marcus was keen to visit Tower Bridge in London because he
  A had heard the changes made to it were amazing.
  B wanted to take his own photos of it.
  C had dreamed of going there for a long time.
  D knew his parents had always wanted to see it.

2 How did Marcus feel before he visited the walkways?
  A unsure whether he was brave enough to go on them
  B confident after what he had read about them online
  C frightened by what his friend had said about them
  D curious to see something he wouldn't find anywhere else

3 How did Marcus feel the first time he crossed the glass sections of the walkways?
  A disappointed with the effect they created
  B entertained by how other people reacted to them
  C worried about walking on the glass
  D annoyed that they were so crowded

4 When the cruise ship passed below the bridge, Marcus was
  A sure he would only see it properly from the bridge.
  B pleased they had planned to stand by the bridge.
  C grateful to see something that rarely happened at the bridge.
  D even more impressed by the ship than the bridge.

5 What would Marcus write on a postcard of Tower Bridge to his grandparents?

  A We all loved walking over the bridge – even Mum, who usually hates going to the top of tall buildings.

  B I hadn't realised that pedestrians aren't allowed to cross the bridge – it's only for cars and lorries.

  C It's amazing that the old bridge can still operate in such an efficient way. I've no idea who looks after it.

  D I hope this reminds you both of where you used to live. Did you use to come here a lot?

6 Work in pairs. Discuss these questions.

1 Would you like to walk across a bridge like the one in the text? Why? / Why not?
2 Do you have any very high bridges or buildings in your country? Where are they? What about in other countries around the world?

Grammar

First & second conditional
Page 92

1 Look at these examples of the first conditional. Then complete the sentences below so they are true for you.

It'**ll be** great **if** our next holiday **is** a cruise to London!
If it's **not** sunny at the weekend, I **won't go** to the beach.
I **might call** you later **if** I **need** help with my homework.

1 If my friends want to go into town after lunch, I
  ....
2 I ....
  if it rains tomorrow.
3 If my mum asks me to go shopping with her, I
  ....
4 I ....
  if I get some money for my birthday.
5 If I don't get my homework finished tonight, I
  ....
6 If .... ,
  I'll ask my dad for some money.

2 Look at these examples of the second conditional. Then complete the sentences below. More than one verb may be possible.

What **would** happen **if** I **didn't manage** it?
I **would be** scared **if** I **saw** a shark!
If I **had** some money, I**'d buy** that T-shirt.

1 If he .... more careful,
  he wouldn't hurt himself so often when he's skateboarding.
2 I .... buy that dress if I were you – it really suits you!
3 If I .... a tiger in the garden, I'd run away!
4 It .... be great if they closed the school because of the snow!
5 Which country would you visit if you .... lots of money?
6 If my favourite film star .... into my classroom, I'd scream!

3 Complete these sentences with the correct form of the verbs in brackets. Add 'll/will, won't, would or wouldn't if necessary.

1 If we don't hurry, we ......'ll miss...... (miss) the bus. We're late!
2 I'd be really sad if I .... (lose) my watch – it was a birthday present from my parents.
3 We probably .... (not go) shopping tomorrow if it snows – it'll be too cold.
4 If we .... (wake up) earlier in the mornings, we wouldn't always be in such a hurry.
5 I .... (not be) very happy if my sister borrowed my clothes without asking.
6 My mum .... (drive) us into town if you don't want to walk.
7 I .... (not watch) that film late at night if I were you – it's really scary!
8 If you come to my house, I .... (help) you make a cake for your mum's birthday.

4 👁 Correct the mistakes in these sentences written by exam candidates. You may be able to correct the sentences in more than one way.

1 We would go shopping if you want, because I love shopping!
2 When I am you, I would go to the large school in the centre of town.
3 What would you do if you find something that you'd lost?
4 I have always wondered what I will say if I saw him again.
5 You are surprised if you come to my room.
6 It would be wonderful if you buy me one of them.

5 Work in pairs. Discuss these questions.

What will you do next weekend if:
1 your best friend isn't free to come out with you?
2 you don't have any money?

How would your life be different if you didn't have access to:
3 a computer?
4 a mobile phone?

Reading

Reading Part 4

✓ **Exam task**

Five sentences have been removed from the text below. For each question, choose the correct answer. There are three extra sentences which you do not need to use.

The Northern Lights in Iceland

What's the most exciting holiday you've ever been on? For me, it was a trip to Iceland with my family to see the Aurora Borealis, or Northern Lights – strange, different-coloured lights that can appear in the night sky. I first became interested in the Northern Lights after watching an amazing video years ago. **1** ____ And now I finally had the chance.

I knew we might not be lucky enough to see the Northern Lights during our visit. **2** ____ But I'd also read that people have a better chance if they find a place with totally dark skies. As a result, going to Iceland during its long, dark winter months seemed a great idea, as there'd be very little sunlight. **3** ____ So that meant temperatures could easily fall to well below zero, which would be difficult to cope with.

However, we weren't going to let any of that spoil our trip. Dad decided it was best to go far away from any cities and stay in the countryside. **4** ____ Anyway, after a long search on the internet, we finally found a hotel miles from anywhere, where the night sky was so dark that we could hardly see anything at all outside!

But then one evening, we suddenly saw the most amazing display of colourful dancing lights in the sky – white, green and even purple in some places. I managed to take some videos even though my hands were almost too cold to operate the camera. **5** ____ So now I have a record of one of the most amazing experiences of my life. And the bonus is that I've visited a really beautiful country, too.

A I thought that was pretty unlikely, though.
B But that was also when the weather would be really bad.
C It wasn't very difficult to achieve.
D It would depend on the weather conditions, for one thing.
E We wanted somewhere with no light pollution from buildings or vehicles.
F We couldn't even get a good view of the stars.
G For that reason, I'd wanted to see them for myself ever since.
H However, I wasn't disappointed with the results I got.

💡 **Exam tip**

Look carefully at what comes **before** and **after** each gap. Read the whole text at the end to check your answers make sense.

TRAVEL & HOLIDAYS

1 Work in pairs. Discuss these questions.

1 Would you like to see the Northern Lights? In which other countries can you see them?
2 Do you prefer lower or higher temperatures? Why?

Listening

Listening Part 2

1 Work in pairs. What are your favourite places to go for a holiday? Look at the photos. Would you enjoy a holiday in these places? Why? / Why not?

2 🔊 33 Look at this exam question and the three options (A, B and C). Listen to the short recording and choose the correct option. Then compare in pairs. Do you agree? Why are the other two options wrong? What key words helped you to find the answer?

You will hear a girl talking to a friend about the place she went to for a holiday.

How did she feel while she was there?

A surprised at how much she learned
B pleased to have her favourite food
C disappointed that there was so little to do

✓ Exam task

🔊 34 For each question, choose the correct answer.

1 You will hear two friends discussing different holidays they've been on.
 What do they agree?
 A Holidays in cities always involve shopping.
 B Holidays by the sea need good weather.
 C Holidays in the mountains offer great activities.

2 You will hear a girl telling a friend about a plane journey she took with her family.
 What was unexpected about it?
 A how quickly they arrived at their destination
 B how soon she ran out of things to do
 C how few passengers there were

3 You will hear a brother and sister talking about their stay at a horse-riding camp.
 How did they both feel about it?
 A disappointed there weren't more people their age
 B surprised at being allowed to go alone
 C impressed by how they were taken care of

💡 Exam tip

You may find it useful to underline key words in the options to help you focus on what you are listening for.

4 You will hear a boy talking to a friend about his photos from a recent trip to a forest.
 What is the girl's opinion of them?
 A They're more interesting than his usual selfies.
 B They were influenced by his teacher.
 C They're much better than he thinks.

5 You will hear a boy asking his friend about good holiday destinations.
 The girl advises him to
 A look for a family adventure park.
 B apply to go to a sports camp.
 C stay somewhere on the coast.

6 You will hear a girl telling her friend about a trip she went on in a submarine.
 Before she went, the girl was
 A worried about the lack of space inside.
 B sure she would enjoy the whole experience.
 C keen to see some fish under the water.

Speaking

Speaking Part 4
>> Pages 112–113

1 Work in pairs. Would you like to try either of the activities in the photos? Why? / Why not?

2 Look at the list of activities in the box. Which would *you* do on holiday if you had the opportunity? Give reasons for your answers.

> cycling   doing extreme sports   doing watersports
> going shopping   going sightseeing
> reading   sleeping   sunbathing
> walking   watching live music

3 🔊 35 Listen to Miguel and Karina answering their teacher's questions about their holidays. Complete these sentences with their answers.

1 I prefer ....
  to ....
2 I like going ....
  more than going ....
3 I'd rather be somewhere ....
  than somewhere ....
4 I don't really enjoy ....
  as much as ....
5 ....
  is much better than ....

4 🔊 35 Listen again. What do Miguel and Karina say about *why* they prefer / don't like different things?

Karina prefers going abroad because it's hot.
Miguel doesn't like ...

💡 Exam tip

- If you don't understand what to do, ask the examiner to repeat the instructions.
- Try to show interest in what your partner says and take turns to speak. Use phrases like *I see* and *Really?*.

✓ Exam task

🔊 36 Work in pairs. Listen to the examiner's questions and take turns to answer when your teacher pauses the recording.

UNIT 8   67

Writing

Writing Part 2
Pages 98–99

1 Work in pairs. Talk about the photo below. Discuss:
- the location
- the weather conditions
- the season
- who's in the photo
- what's happening

2 The photo was taken by a boy called Lee during his holiday. Now his teacher has asked him to do the exam task below and write about his photo.

Read Lee's article. He has made some mistakes. Find five spelling mistakes, five punctuation mistakes and four grammar mistakes. Then compare in pairs.

> You see this announcement in an international magazine.
>
> **Articles wanted!**
>
> **WHAT'S THE BEST HOLIDAY PHOTO YOU'VE EVER TAKEN?**
>
> Tell us about where you were when you took the photo, what happened, and how you felt about your photo at the time you took it.
>
> **Write an article answering these questions and we will publish the most interesting articles in our magazine.**
>
> Write your **article** in about **100 words**.

i've always taken loads of photos during my holydays, with the phone on my camera. Theyre great to look at when you come home, and remmember where you were – and its even better if you can photograph something really unusual.

Anyway, during my last holiday, I was walked along a road in croatia where there was a lots of water. Sudenly I saw a boy waterskiing along the road it was amazing!

So I quickly take a foto and I was really pleased the result. In fact, I entered it in a competion – and I actually won!

68

Writing

3 Read these sentences with the past simple and past continuous. Then complete the rules below.

*I **was walking** along the road when I **saw** a man.*

*My phone **rang** while I **was cycling** to football practice.*

1. In the examples, the .... is used to talk about the long action – the one that began first.
2. The .... is used to talk about the short action – the one that began second.

4 Complete the sentences below with the past simple or past continuous of the verbs in brackets.

1. I was cycling to school when I .... (see) my cat in a tree.
2. I .... (walk) through the zoo when I saw a crocodile coming towards me!
3. I .... (eat) an ice cream when my phone rang.
4. I lost my money while I .... (sit) on the bus.
5. I was talking on my mobile when my friend .... (arrive).
6. The students .... (all / talk) when the teacher .... (walk) in.
7. What .... (you / do) when I rang you at eight last night?
8. When I saw my friend in town, he .... (buy) a new T-shirt in a shop.

5 In his article in Exercise 2, Lee wrote *I saw a boy waterskiing.* Complete these sentences in the same way.

1. When I went into the classroom, I heard ....
2. When I walked into the café, I saw ....

6 Work in pairs. Discuss these questions.

1. Have you ever seen anything strange or amazing on holiday?
2. Have you got a photo that you're very proud of, or that you like for a special reason? Describe it to your partner.
3. How often do you take photos?
4. What do you usually take photos of?
5. Is it important to take photos, especially on holiday? Why? / Why not?
6. Have you got any photos of when you were very young? Describe them.

✓ Exam task

You see this announcement on an international photography website.

> **Articles wanted!**
>
> **A FAVOURITE PHOTO**
>
> *What's your favourite photo?*
>
> *It could be a photo that you or your family took, or one that you've seen somewhere.*
>
> *Tell us what the photo is of, what was happening when the photo was taken, and why you like it so much.*
>
> **Write an article answering these questions and we will publish the most interesting articles on our website.**

Write your **article** in about **100** words.

💡 Exam tip

Try to learn as many phrases as possible from sample answers and use them in your writing.

UNIT 8

Revision

UNIT 1

1 Choose the correct form of the verbs: present simple or present continuous.

1 Jack *sits / is sitting* in the living room at the moment, doing his homework.
2 Paul *is getting up / gets up* at 7.00 a.m. on school mornings.
3 *We come / We're coming* from Spain, but *we live / we're living* in Canada for a year.
4 Sarah *says / is saying* her dad *cooks / is cooking* the family dinner every Sunday.
5 Peter *really wants / is really wanting* to see the latest sci-fi film at the cinema.
6 Holly's sister *is / is being* a student at university, but *she's working / she works* in a supermarket this summer.
7 *I don't enjoy / I'm not enjoying* this book very much – it's quite boring.
8 *Do you like / Are you liking* chocolate ice cream?

2 Complete these sentences with the correct prepositions.

1 Anna and Lucy are looking forward .... going to the mountains because they love skiing.
2 Matteo doesn't want to go climbing because he's afraid .... falling.
3 My sister can help you with your homework – she's really good .... explaining difficult topics.
4 Nathan is an excellent swimmer, so he's interested .... learning to surf.

3 Match the definitions below of different places in a school with the words/phrases in the box.

> canteen   classroom   gym   hall   IT room   playground   reception
> science lab   sports field   tennis courts

1 This is where you can play sports indoors. ....
2 The students and staff eat their lunch here. ....
3 You can find computers and printers in this room. ....
4 If you have to carry out an experiment, you go here. ....
5 Students can play football, rugby and hockey here. ....
6 This is an outside space that students use during break time. ....
7 Most of the school day is spent here. ....
8 If there is a big event or meeting, lots of classes can sit together in this place. ....
9 This is the place in the school where people go when they first arrive. ....
10 You go here to play a game with a ball and a racket. ....

4 Choose the correct verbs.

1 In our school, we have to *wear / take* a uniform. It's blue and grey.
2 When Nancy changed school, she didn't know anyone, so she decided to *take up / join* an after-school club to meet some new friends.
3 Most of my classmates eat in the school canteen, but I prefer to *attend / eat* a packed lunch because I don't like the school lunches.
4 My mum said if I *take / get* good grades this year, she'll buy me a new phone, so I'm working really hard!
5 Louis's maths teacher was not pleased when he *handed in / joined* his homework late.
6 Julia wasn't good enough for the volleyball team, so she's hoping to *perform / take up* a new sport next year.
7 We visited the science museum last week. Are you *attending / going* on a school trip this term?
8 The students in the fourth year can't watch the sports competition because they have to *take / perform* exams next week.

/30

Revision

UNIT 2

1 Complete these sentences with the past simple of the verbs in brackets.

1. What time .... (the film / finish) last night?
2. Sandra .... (buy) a new bag for her weekend trip to Dublin.
3. Alex and Paul .... (be) really happy because they .... (pass) the exam.
4. Antonia .... (not like) the music at the party, so she .... (not dance).
5. Where .... (you / go) on holiday last year?
6. My sister .... (want) to invite her friends to the cinema yesterday.

2 Choose the correct form of the verbs: past simple or past continuous.

1. Alison *stopped / was stopping* listening to music when her friend *arrived / was arriving*.
2. Patrick *lost / was losing* his exercise book when he *cycled / was cycling* to school.
3. My grandmother *waited / was waiting* for the bus when she *saw / was seeing* her friend.
4. The boys *ate / were eating* ice cream when it *started / was starting* to rain.
5. What *did you see / were you seeing* when you *went / were going* to Athens?
6. My mum *worked / was working* in the garden when she *hurt / was hurting* her back.

3 Choose the correct words (A, B or C) to complete these sentences.

1. It's important to work hard if you want to .... in your exams.
   A achieve   B succeed   C win

2. Very few people are lucky enough to .... all their dreams.
   A succeed   B win   C achieve

3. We .... the other team by six goals to one!
   A beat   B won   C succeeded

4. Sally was very upset when she .... the race against her sister.
   A defeated   B lost   C beat

5. The last time we .... the championship was in 2015.
   A beat   B won   C achieved

6. I don't mind being .... if I feel the other team deserves to win.
   A defeated   B lost   C won

4 Complete these sentences with the verbs in the box.

> believe   get   give   hand   join   stay

1. I'm really tired, so I'm not going to the party tonight – I'm going to .... in.
2. When we got to the cinema it was full, so we couldn't .... in.
3. If you want to be a champion, you must never .... in.
4. It's very important to .... in yourself if you want to be successful.
5. Emily's alone over there. Ask her if she wants to .... in with the game.
6. The teacher asked the students to .... in their homework on Monday morning.

5 Complete these sentences by adding the correct ending to the words.

1. I was so happy when our class won the school chess compet.................... .
2. I'm not usually very compet...................., but it was the first time we had won anything!
3. Jane is the best athl.................... in the school. She was selected for the national champ.................... .
4. My favourite sport is athl.................... . Usain Bolt is my hero!
5. When she was a child, Marie wasn't very athl...................., but she became a champ.................... swimmer when she was 19.
6. How many compet.................... were in that race?

/30

Revision

UNIT 3

1 Complete these sentences with the correct form of the adjectives in brackets. Add other words if necessary.

1 Clothes at the open-air market are usually .... (cheap) clothes you buy in department stores.
2 Our secondary school is .... (big) in town – there are 900 students here.
3 What can I do if I want to get a .... (good) mark in the next English test than I did in the last one?
4 I wanted to buy the blue dress, but it is .... (expensive) the skirt, so I'm not sure.
5 Jane is .... (fashionable) girl I know – she always wears the latest style.
6 I love doing science experiments at school. It's much .... (interesting) learning from a book.
7 My parents bought me a new bed last week. It's .... (comfortable) my old one.
8 We were .... (bad) team in the tournament. We lost every match!

2 Choose the correct words (A, B or C) to complete these sentences.

1 That new .... goes perfectly with your dress.
  A sleeve   B necklace   C gloves

2 I needed a dark suit for the interview, so I chose a .... one.
  A navy-blue   B cream   C silver

3 The .... on my shoe broke when I ran for the bus. It was so embarrassing!
  A collar   B heel   C button

4 My brother asked for a pair of .... for his birthday because he wanted to start running in the park.
  A sandals   B earrings   C trainers

5 You should put on a .... It's cold outside today.
  A T-shirt   B skirt   C jumper

6 Pablo likes to find unusual clothes, so he sometimes buys his clothes in a ....
  A department store
  B second-hand shop
  C traditional shop

3 Complete the words for these definitions.

1 You wear this on your finger: r....................
2 Shoes, bags and jackets can be made from this material: l....................
3 Clothes which are comfortable and not smart: c....................
4 The material most summer clothes are made from: c....................
5 Jewellery made from this metal is very expensive: g....................
6 A jacket and trousers which go together: s....................
7 A natural material which is used for winter clothes: w....................
8 Two colours which start with the letter *p*: p.................... and p....................

4 Write the adjectives in the correct order to complete these sentences.

1 I would like a .... (gold / new / smart) bracelet for my birthday.
2 Justine bought a .... (cotton / light-blue / beautiful) top last weekend.
3 My new jacket has .... (cream / small / stylish) buttons on the sleeves.
4 Karl's wearing .... (dark-red / casual) trainers at school today.
5 Can I borrow your .... (wool / pink / comfortable) jumper?
6 Let's look at the .... (online / fashionable) shop.

/28

Revision

UNIT 4

1 Choose the correct form of the verbs: present perfect or past simple.

1. *I've never been / I never went* to Paris. I hope to go there soon.
2. *Did Ray go / Has Ray been* to the cinema last Saturday?
3. How long *have you known / did you know* your best friend?
4. When *have you met / did you meet* Sophie for the first time?
5. *We've had / We had* our dog since 2010.
6. This is the first time *they ever ate / they've ever eaten* sushi.
7. *My brother's always wanted / My brother always wanted* to go to the adventure theme park, so my mum's taking him there for his birthday next month.
8. Where *did your teacher find / has your teacher found* your glasses?

2 Choose the correct words.

1. I've lived in this house *for / since* I was born.
2. We haven't been to the cinema *for / since* a long time because the one in our town closed down last year.
3. My mum has worked at the bank *for / since* she graduated from university.
4. Karl has known his best friend *for / since* seven years – they met at primary school.
5. I've been here *for / since* 25 minutes! Where have you been?
6. Jenny and Pauline have studied French *for / since* they were ten years old.

3 Complete the sentences below with the adjectives in the box.

> disappointed   excited   jealous   surprised   worried

1. **A:** Are you .... about the party next week?
   B: Yes, I can't wait!
2. I didn't enjoy that film. I was .... because that actor is usually so funny.
3. My sister was .... because I went to the music festival with my friends and she had to stay at home.
4. Kate is quite .... about the maths test next week because she finds maths very difficult.
5. Paul's never won anything in his life, so he was really .... when they announced his name.

4 Choose the correct adjectives.

1. Diane wasn't *satisfied / annoyed* with her exam results, so she's going to try to do better next time.
2. Sometimes I'm *afraid / jealous* of my classmate because she's so confident and I'm quite shy.
3. Are you *serious / impressed* about wanting to be a doctor? You'll have to work very hard.
4. I'm the best player in the team, so I'm not *anxious / annoyed* about the match on Saturday.
5. I was *annoyed / amazed* when I passed my music exam – I hardly did any practice for it.

5 Complete the phrasal verbs in these sentences.

1. Have you ever taken .... in a talent show?
2. Would you like to take .... a new sport?
3. Last year, the event took .... in the local park.

/27

Revision

UNIT 5

1 Choose the correct form of the verb (A, B or C) to complete these sentences.

1 This summer I .... to spend three weeks in Ireland because I want to improve my English.
  A 'm going   B will go   C go

2 Do you think you .... to university when you finish school?
  A are going   B will go   C go

3 It's late! I .... my train!
  A 'm missing   B 'll miss   C miss

4 What time .... the concert tomorrow?
  A is being   B will be   C is

2 Choose the correct form of the verbs.

1 A: The maths homework is really difficult. I don't understand it.
   B: *I'll / I'm going to* help you. I've already finished it.

2 A: Are you going shopping?
   B: Yes, *I'll / I'm going to* buy a new shirt for the party on Saturday.

3 A: I'm sure Caroline *will win / is winning* the tennis match this afternoon.
   B: Yes, she's the best player in the school.

4 A: Oh no! I left my pencil case at home!
   B: Don't worry, *I'll / I'm going* to lend you a pen.

5 A: Katy broke her leg when she went skiing last week.
   B: I know. *I'll / I'm going* to visit her tomorrow.

6 A: Those children are playing a dangerous game.
   B: Yes, I think *they'll / they're going to* fall.

3 Complete the words for these definitions.

1 a small soft red fruit: s.... ....
2 a long orange vegetable: c.... ....
3 a vegetable with very dark green leaves that you can eat cooked or uncooked: s.... ....
4 a large fruit which has a rough orange or brown skin and pointed leaves and which grows in hot countries: p.... ....
5 a vegetable with large, green leaves which is used in salads: l.... ....
6 a small round green or purple fruit that you can eat or make into wine: g.... ....
7 a round sweet fruit with a lot of juice and a soft yellow or pink skin: p.... ....
8 a long vegetable made of yellow seeds: c.... ....

4 Complete the sentences below with the words in the box.

| beef | chicken | cod | lamb | salmon | tuna | turkey |

1 People often eat .... at Christmas in the UK and at Thanksgiving in the US.
2 Some people prefer to eat less red meat these days, so they choose white meat such as .... or turkey.
3 .... is a fish which is silver on the outside and pink inside.
4 .... is the meat from a cow. It is often used to make burgers.
5 In some countries, they eat .... at Easter. It's meat from a baby sheep.
6 .... is a large fish. You can buy it fresh, frozen or in tins.
7 .... is a fish which is white inside. It is traditionally eaten with chips in the UK.

5 Add the missing letters to complete these definitions.

1 F.... .... food is kept at a temperature below 0°C.
2 R.... .... food is uncooked.
3 F.... .... food is cooked in oil.
4 B.... .... vegetables are cooked in very hot water.

6 Complete these sentences with the correct prepositions.

1 They put the fire .... very quickly, so there wasn't any damage.
2 Andrew put .... weight when he stopped walking to school every day.
3 My dad says my bedroom looks terrible because I never put my clothes ....
4 I've asked my teacher to put my name .... for the theatre trip next week.
5 It was raining, so they had to put .... the school sports day.
6 The swimming pool has put .... its prices, so I'm going to try playing badminton instead because it's cheaper.

/35

Revision

UNIT 6

1 Complete these sentences with the correct form of *used to*.

1 Dan .... play the guitar in a band, but he doesn't have time for it now.
2 When my grandfather was young, he .... have a car, so he walked everywhere.
3 .... play football with your brother when you were younger?
4 There .... be four bookshops in our town, but now there's only one because a lot of people buy books online.
5 I .... like spinach when I was a child, but it's my favourite vegetable now.
6 We .... live in Oxford, but we moved to Bristol two years ago because my dad changed his job.

2 Complete the second sentence of each pair so that it means the same as the first.

1 'You should take a coat with you, Karl,' said his mum.
  Karl's mum advised .... a coat.
2 'I'm sorry I forgot your birthday,' said Tina.
  Tina apologised .... Grace's birthday.
3 'I'll help you with your homework if you like, Jack,' said his father.
  Jack's father offered .... Jack with his homework.
4 I don't know what it would be like to live in the mountains.
  I can't imagine .... in the mountains.
5 'I'll take you to football practice tomorrow, Harry,' said Dad.
  Harry's dad promised .... to football practice the next day.
6 Will's mum never travels home from work at 5 p.m., as there's so much traffic then.
  Will's mum always avoids .... home from work at 5 p.m. because of the traffic.
7 'Why don't we go swimming tomorrow?' said Tom.
  Tom suggested .... swimming the following day.
8 Richard's dad is buying him a car as soon as he's old enough to drive.
  Richard's dad intends .... a car as soon as he's old enough to drive.

3 Complete these sentences with the correct form of *do, make, have* or *go*.

1 Our school is going to .... a Christmas party this year.
2 My parents always .... shopping on Saturday afternoon.
3 Michael and Alan enjoy .... fishing at the lake during the holidays.
4 I'm sorry I can't come out this evening – I still have to .... my homework.
5 The school team are .... a rugby match on Friday. Do you want to go and watch?
6 I couldn't concentrate on reading my book because my little sister and her friends were .... a noise.

4 Choose the correct words.

1 The highest *mountain / lake* in the world is Everest.
2 The tram stops just in front of the school, so it's quite *comfortable / convenient* for the students.
3 My aunt prefers to visit *peaceful / crowded* places, so she usually goes to the countryside on holiday.
4 We often go to my grandma's house at the weekend. It's not very big, but it is *huge / cosy*.
5 Carlotta likes visiting historical buildings, so last Saturday she went to the nearby *coast / castle*.
6 The hotel is next to the *forest / beach*, so you can take a swim whenever you like.
7 We climbed to the top of the hill and had a great *view / space* of the city.
8 The summer camp is great fun. There are lots of activities like sailing and singing lessons and you can go dancing in the evenings – it's very *freezing / lively*.
9 The best part of the holiday was the river trip through the *desert / jungle*.
10 We live in a flat, so we don't have a garden, but we have got a big *balcony / countryside*.

/30

Revision

UNIT 7

1 Complete these sentences with the past simple or past perfect of the verbs in brackets.

1. Marcus .... (not be) hungry because he .... (just have) lunch.
2. I .... (never eat) curry before I .... (go) to that Indian restaurant last week.
3. When Julie .... (arrive) at the station the train .... (already leave).
4. Tina .... (never receive) an invitation to a ball before, so she .... (not know) what to wear.
5. Alfie and Sarah .... (look) very well because they .... (just come back) from a holiday in Greece.
6. It .... (be) the first time John .... (go) ice-skating, but he was very good at it.

2 Complete the second sentence of each pair using direct speech.

1. He said he'd never seen a snake before.
   'I .... a snake before.'
2. My teacher said we would do a project on the environment next week.
   'We .... a project on the environment next week.'
3. She asked me if I had a pet.
   '.................... a pet?'
4. Jack told me he was going on holiday on Friday.
   'I .... on holiday on Friday.'
5. She wanted to know where I'd bought my camera.
   'Where .... your camera?'
6. The teacher told us not to use our mobile phones in school.
   'Please .... your mobile phones in school.'

3 Match the animal definitions below with the words in the box.

| bat | camel | elephant | gorilla | parrot | penguin |
| shark | snake | spider | whale |

1. A small animal like a mouse which flies at night:
   ....
2. A large animal with four legs and two humps which lives in the desert:
   ....
3. A big, grey animal with a long nose:
   ....
4. A tropical bird which is usually very colourful:
   ....
5. A creature with eight legs:
   ....
6. A very large sea mammal that breathes through a hole at the top of its head:
   ....
7. A sea bird which cannot fly:
   ....
8. A large fish with a lot of sharp teeth:
   ....
9. A very big creature from central Africa which looks like a monkey:
   ....
10. A long, thin animal which doesn't have legs:
    ....

4 Complete the sentences below with the words in the box. You will not need all of them.

clear	cruel	freezing	frozen	humid	ice
jungle	litter	ocean	oil	pollution	protect
rare	sunset	waterfall

1. The .... we are creating is destroying the planet and some people think it is creating global warming.
2. My favourite thing about being on holiday is relaxing on the beach at the end of the day and looking at the colours of the ....
3. You can see some .... animals in wildlife parks and zoos.
4. Yesterday it snowed all day. It was .... !
5. We need to do more to .... animals such as tigers and gorillas.
6. It was Environment Week last week at school, so our class went to the local park to clean up the .... that people had left.
7. Alice saw a spectacular .... in the mountains last weekend, but she got wet when she walked too near it.
8. People must reduce the amount of plastic in the .... because fish and other sea animals are dying.
9. They saw some very unusual animals and plants on their tour of the .... in Costa Rica.
10. I think it's .... to keep animals in cages in a zoo. They don't look happy and should live in their natural environment.

/32

Revision

UNIT 8

1 Choose the correct form of the verbs.

1 I want to be in the basketball team. If I *practise / will practise* every day, do you think the coach *selects / will select* me?
2 My grandmother told me she *takes / will take* me to London for the weekend if I *do / will do* well in my exams.
3 *Do you help / Will you help* me tidy my bedroom if I *give / will give* you some money?
4 If it *snows / will snow* this weekend we *will / wouldn't* go skiing.
5 My brother *drives / will drive* me to school next week if he *passes / will pass* his driving test at the weekend.
6 It's seven o'clock! If I *will run / don't run*, I *miss / 'll miss* the last bus home.

2 Choose the correct verbs (A, B or C) to complete these sentences.

1 If trains .... so expensive, more people would use them to go to work and there would be less traffic on the roads.
   A weren't   B wouldn't   C were
2 You're always tired! If you didn't go to bed so late, you .... be tired all the time.
   A won't   B wouldn't   C would
3 Which country would you like to visit if you .... enough money?
   A have   B had   C hadn't
4 If I .... you, I wouldn't buy that DVD. That film is on TV tonight.
   A was   B would be   C were
5 If your teacher asked you to make a presentation about your hobby, what .... you talk about?
   A will   B did   C would
6 If you .... a lost dog in the park, what would you do?
   A find   B would find   C found
7 What would you say if James .... you to his party?
   A invited   B invite   C invites
8 How .... you feel if you couldn't find your mobile phone?
   A will   B would   C did

3 Complete these sentences.

1 Drivers have to stop when the t.................... l.................... turn red.
2 There were lots of yachts and small boats in the h.................... .
3 Passengers are waiting on the p.................... for their train.
4 A p.................... is the person who flies a plane.
5 The bus was so c.................... that no one could get on or off.
6 Vehicles are allowed to drive faster on a m.................... than on other roads.
7 You can either c.................... i.................... online or at the airport.
8 Don't forget to wear your s.................... b.................... when you travel on a plane or in a car.
9 Travelling by boat can be unpleasant if there are big w.................... .
10 You cannot get on a plane if you don't show your b.................... p.................... .

4 Choose the correct words.

Last August, we flew to Málaga in Spain for our summer holiday. The journey started badly when we got stuck in a (1) *traffic jam / traffic lights* on the way to the (2) *airport / harbour*. Then, my dad couldn't find the entrance to the car park, so he drove round the (3) *motorway / roundabout* three times! Finally, we arrived at the check-in desk, but I had forgotten to (4) *weigh / land* my bag, so I had to pay an extra £10 because it was too heavy. Then, we were stopped at (5) *security / station* because my sister had a bottle of water in her bag. She quickly threw the bottle in the bin and we ran to the (6) *pilot / gate*, showed our boarding passes and waited for the plane to (7) *check in / take off*. The flight was (8) *rough / efficient* because there was a storm over the mountains, so we were really happy when it was time to (9) *land / take off*. Luckily, the rest of the holiday was fantastic.

/33

Grammar reference

UNIT 1
Modals (1)

have to, must

- We use *have to* and *must* to express obligation:
  We **have to show** our passports when we cross the border.
  You **must take** your passport with you everywhere you go.
- We often use *have to* to talk about rules or laws which were made by someone else or which we may not agree with:
  My teacher says that I **have to finish** the homework tonight or I'll be in trouble.
- We often use *must* to talk about rules or laws which we agree with or believe in:
  We **must wear** a seat belt in the car, even for short journeys.

don't have to

We use *don't have to* (but not *mustn't*) when it is not necessary to do something:
We **didn't have to show** our passports when we crossed into Scotland.

mustn't

- We use *mustn't* to express prohibition, to say that something is not allowed:
  You **mustn't use** your phone in the cinema.
- We can also use *can't* instead of *mustn't*:
  You **can't talk** during the exam.
- There is no past tense of *mustn't*. We use *not allowed to*:
  We **weren't allowed to go** into the concert without a ticket.

can/can't

We can also use *can/can't* to express permission or lack of permission:
You **can leave** any time you like.
You **can't bring** animals in here.
Can I use your phone, please?

should/shouldn't

- We use *should/shouldn't* to give or ask for advice. *Should/shouldn't* is followed by the infinitive without *to*:
  You **should join** a gym if you want to keep fit.
  You **shouldn't eat** too much chocolate.
  What **should I do**?
- An alternative to *should* is *ought to* + infinitive. It is not usually used in negative sentences or questions:
  You **ought to join** a gym if you want to keep fit.

Practice

1 Complete these sentences with *can/can't*, *must* or *mustn't*.

1 We .... bring a dog in here.

2 We .... pay in cash. We .... pay by credit card.

3 We .... use wi-fi here.

4 We .... sit at this table. It's reserved.

5 We .... use our phones here.

2 Choose the correct verbs.

When my grandfather was young, children **(1)** *must not / didn't have to* stay at school until the age of 18 or even 16. They **(2)** *could / couldn't* leave when they were 14. My grandfather, for example, had no choice. He **(3)** *had to / didn't have to* go out and work to earn money for his family. At the end of every week, he **(4)** *could / had to* give his wages to his mother. She gave him a small amount of pocket money, which he **(5)** *had to / could* spend as he liked. When he was 18, he wanted to join the army, but unfortunately, he failed the medical examination, so he **(6)** *had to / didn't have to* do military service. This meant he couldn't fight for his country. Instead of being a soldier like all his friends, he drove an ambulance.

Present simple & present continuous

Present simple

Positive/Negative forms		
I/You/We/They	**take**	photos.
	do not / don't take	
He/She/It	**takes**	
	does not / doesn't take	

Question forms			
Do	I/you/we/they	**take**	photos?
Does	he/she/it		

Short answers		
Yes,	I/you/we/they	**do**.
	he/she/it	**does**.
No,	I/you/we/they	**don't**.
	he/she/it	**doesn't**.

We can use the present simple to talk about something that …
- is generally true and permanent at the present time:
  My brother **lives** in France.
- is a fact or is always true:
  The sun **rises** in the east.
- happens regularly:
  I **play** tennis every Tuesday.

Present continuous

Positive/Negative forms		
I	am/'m	
	am/'m not	
You/We/They	are/'re	**working** at the moment.
	are not / aren't / 're not	
He/She/It	is/'s	
	is not / isn't / 's not	

Question forms & short answers		
Am	I	**working** at the moment?
Are	you/we/they	
Is	he/she/it	
Yes,	I	**am**.
	you/we/they	**are**.
	he/she/it	**is**.
No,	I	**am/'m not**.
	you/we/they	**aren't / 're not**.
	he/she/it	**isn't / 's not**.

We can use the present continuous to talk about …
- something happening now:
  I**'m watching** a film on TV.
- a temporary situation which is true now:
  They**'re living** with friends while their house is being repaired.
- something happening in the present but not necessarily at that moment:
  My sister**'s studying** art at college.

Practice

3 Choose the correct form of the verbs: present simple or present continuous.

Many people **(1)** *take up / are taking up* cycling these days. Cycling is great because it **(2)** *helps / is helping* our general fitness. When we cycle, we **(3)** *use up / are using up* more energy than when we **(4)** *walk / are walking*. **(5)** *I go / I'm going* cycling regularly, but only on small roads where there aren't many cars. At the moment, **(6)** *I train / I'm training* for a race, so **(7)** *I spend / I'm spending* a lot of time on my bike.

State verbs

State verbs refer to a state or a condition, rather than an action. They are not normally used with continuous verbs:
✓ I **prefer** apples to oranges.
✗ I'm preferring apples to oranges.

GRAMMAR REFERENCE 79

- Here is a list of common state verbs:

agree appear believe depend hear hope know like look love need own possess prefer see seem smell suppose taste think understand want weigh wish

- There are verbs which can be both state verbs and action verbs, but which have a different meaning:
  She **looks** tired. (*look* = appear)
  She**'s looking** for her phone. (*look* = search)
  He **has** an apartment. (*have* = own)
  He**'s having** breakfast. (*have* = eat)

Practice

4 Complete these sentences with the present simple or present continuous of the verbs in the box.

cost have help own prefer smell think want weigh

1 **A:** How much .... you .... , Ben?
   B: I don't know. About 60 kilos, maybe?
   I .... not to know, actually.
2 Paul is a computer expert. He .... people with their IT problems.
3 The flowers in our garden .... beautiful.
4 My dad .... a lot of problems with his car at the moment.
5 A cinema ticket .... €15! I .... that's a lot of money!
6 Lucas .... a new bike, but he .... to sell it.

-ing forms

- After verbs of liking, such as *like / don't like, enjoy, hate, dislike, don't mind, love, fancy, feel like, can't stand*, etc., the *-ing* form of the following verb is usually used:

I **hate doing** the washing-up.
I **love going** to the cinema.

- *-ing* forms are also used after most prepositions:
I'm good **at dancing**.
I'm interested **in learning** Spanish.

Practice

5 Complete this conversation with the correct present simple, present continuous or *-ing* form of the verbs in brackets.

A: What **(1)** .... you .... (do)?
B: I **(2)** .... (fill in) a form about my likes and dislikes to find a new e-pal.
A: Oh, OK. Shall I read out the questions?
B: Yes, please.
A: Right. Do you enjoy **(3)** .... (meet) friends after school?
B: I love **(4)** .... (hang out) with my friends.
I **(5)** .... (meet) them every afternoon after school.
A: And do you like **(6)** .... (do) sports?
B: To be honest, I can't stand **(7)** .... (do) sports. I'm really lazy!
A: Final question. **(8)** .... you .... (like) listening to music?
B: Yes, I love listening to all types of music, except for jazz.
A: OK. Do you fancy **(9)** .... (watch) a film at the cinema later? There are some good films on at the moment.
B: No, thanks, I **(10)** .... (not feel like) going out tonight.

UNIT 2

Past simple

be

	Positive/Negative forms	
I/He/She/It	was	here yesterday.
	was not / wasn't	
You/We/They	were	
	were not / weren't	

Question forms & short answers		
Was	I/he/she/it	here yesterday?
Were	you/we/they	
Yes,	I/he/she/it	was.
	you/we/they	were.
No,	I/he/she/it	wasn't.
	you/we/they	weren't.

Other verbs

play (regular)
go (irregular)

	Positive/Negative forms	
I/You/We/They/He/She/It	**played** did not play / didn't play	tennis yesterday.
	went did not go / didn't go	to school yesterday.

Question forms & short answers				
Did	I/you/we/they/he/she/it	**play**	tennis yesterday?	
		go	to school yesterday?	
Yes,	I/you/we/they/he/she/it	**did**.		
No,	I/you/we/they/he/she/it	**didn't**.		

Spelling of regular past simple verbs

For regular verbs, we add *-ed* to the base form of the verb, or *-d* if the verb already ends in *-e*:

attract → attract**ed**   help → help**ed**   arrive → arrive**d**

For verbs ending in:	Present simple	Past simple
• a consonant + *-y*, change the *y* to *i* and add *-ed*.	study carry	stud**ied** carr**ied**
• a vowel + a consonant (with stress on last syllable), double the final consonant and add *-ed*.	plan prefer drop	pla**nned** prefe**rred** dro**pped**
• a vowel + a consonant (with no stress on the last syllable), add *-ed*.	happen develop visit	happen**ed** develop**ed** visit**ed**
• a vowel + *-l*, double the *l* and add *-ed*.	travel control	trave**lled** contro**lled**

We use the past simple to talk about …
- past actions/events/states which have finished:
  Jenny **was** tired after she **went** ice skating.
- repeated past actions:
  I **cycled** to school every day when I was a student.
- a sequence of past actions:
  We **left** home, **walked** to the station and **caught** the train.

Past continuous

	Positive/Negative forms	
I/He/She/It	**was** was not / wasn't	studying all evening.
You/We/They	**were** were not / weren't	

Question forms & short answers		
Was	I/he/she/it	**studying** all evening?
Were	you/we/they	
Yes,	I/he/she/it	**was**.
	you/we/they	**were**.
No,	I/he/she/it	**wasn't**.
	you/we/they	**weren't**.

We use the past continuous to talk about …
- a particular moment in the past:
  Emily **was walking** the dog at 5 p.m.
- temporary actions which give extra (less important) information:
  It **was raining**, so I decided not to go out.
- two or more actions happening at the same time:
  While I **was doing** my homework, my brother **was playing** the guitar.
- an action happening when another action happened:
  He **was cleaning** his bike when he hurt his hand.

when, while & as

We can use these words with the past continuous to introduce an action happening at the same time as another:
When Joe was walking home, it started to rain.
The phone rang **while** I was having breakfast.
They arrived **as** we were leaving.

Practice

1 Choose the correct form of the verbs: past simple or past continuous.

1. While I *watched / was watching* TV, my sister was doing her homework.
2. My friends *often phoned / were often phoning* me when my parents were out.
3. While I was talking to my friend, I *realised / was realising* that something was wrong.
4. It was a lovely day. The sun *shone / was shining* and the birds *sang / were singing*.
5. Mo Farah *won / was winning* a gold medal for Great Britain in the Rio Olympics.

2 Complete these sentences with the past simple or past continuous of the verbs in brackets.

1. While I .... (tidy) my room, I .... (find) some old photographs.
2. As I .... (leave) the cinema, I .... (realise) that I'd left my phone behind.
3. While Simon .... (watch) television, his brother .... (cook) dinner.
4. When we .... (hear) the fire alarm, we all .... (stop) what we .... (do) and .... (walk) out of the building.
5. My computer .... (crash) while I .... (update) my web page.

UNIT 3

Order of adjectives

- The usual order of adjectives before a noun is: **opinion / size / shape / age / colour / nationality / material / type + object**
- But we do not often use more than three adjectives before a noun:
  a **beautiful big red** bag
  an **interesting new Italian** film
- Numbers always go before other adjectives:
  He's got **two** clever older sisters.
- With two or more adjectives referring to colour, use *and*:
  a blue **and** white T-shirt
  an orange, white **and** red flag

Practice

1 Write these adjectives in the correct order.

1. a/an *pretty old blue* shirt (old / pretty / blue)
2. a/an .... car (old / Spanish / lovely)
3. a .... flag (red / Danish / white / new)
4. a .... skirt (blue / cotton / short)
5. a/an .... novel (historical / long / interesting)
6. my .... jacket (leather / favourite / blue)

Comparative & superlative adjectives

- We use comparative adjectives (e.g. *bigger than*) to compare two people or things and to say if one has more of a quality (e.g. size, height, etc.) than the other.
- Comparative adjectives are usually followed by *than*.
- We use superlative adjectives (e.g. *the fastest, the most important*) to say that in a particular group, something has the most of a quality.

Regular adjectives

		Comparative	Superlative
•	For most adjectives, add *-er* or *-est*.	small → small**er** Italy is **smaller** than Spain.	small → **the** small**est** Vatican City is **the smallest** country in the world.
•	For short adjectives ending in *-e*, add *-r* or *-st*.	large → larg**er** Canada is **larger** than China.	large → **the** larg**est** Russia is **the largest** country in the world.
•	For short adjectives ending in a vowel + a consonant, double the consonant and add *-er* or *-est*.	hot → hot**ter** Algeria is **hotter** than Mexico.	hot → **the** hot**test** Libya is one of **the hottest** countries in the world.
•	For two-syllable adjectives ending in *-y*, change the *y* to *i* and add *-er* or *-est*.	heavy → heav**ier** Elephants are **heavier** than crocodiles.	→ **the** heav**iest** Blue whales are **the heaviest** animals in the world.
•	For some two-syllable adjectives, we can either add *-er/-est* or use *more / the most*. These are adjectives ending in *-ow*, *-le*, *-er* and *polite*, *quiet*, *common* and *stupid*.	Mia is **more polite** than me. = Mia is **politer** than me.	Mia is **the most polite** girl in the class. = Mia is **the politest** girl in the class.
•	For longer adjectives, or two-syllable adjectives ending in *-ful*, put *more/less* and *the most/ least* before the adjective.	difficult → **more/ less** difficult Some people think it's **more difficult** to make friends when you are older.	difficult → **the most/least** difficult Is it true that Japanese is **the most difficult** language for English speakers to learn?

82

Irregular adjectives

There are three irregular adjectives – *good, bad, far*:
good → better → the best
bad → worse → the worst
far → farther/further* → the farthest/furthest*

* There is no difference in meaning, but *further / the furthest* is more common.

(not) as … as

- We use *as* + adjective/adverb + *as* to say that two things are the same:
  Hannah is **as tall as** Jess.
  Today is **as warm as** yesterday.
- We use *not as* + adjective/adverb + *as* to say that one thing is less than another:
  My brother is**n't as fit as** me. = I am fitter than my brother.
  I'm **not as fast as** my brother. = My brother is faster than me.

Practice

2 Complete these comparative and superlative adjectives.

1	thin	thinner than	....
2	bad	.... than	the worst
3	....	lazier than	the laziest
4	comfortable	.... than	the most comfortable
5	good	better than	....
6	nice	.... than	the nicest
7	....	farther/further than	the farthest/furthest

3 Complete these sentences with the comparative or superlative form of the adjectives in brackets.

1 It rained every day in December 2015 in Portland, USA. It was .... (wet) December for 75 years.
2 We've moved house. Now we live .... (far) from my school than we used to.
3 A blue whale is .... (heavy) than an elephant.
4 I felt ill all weekend, but I'm much .... (good) now.
5 This writer's new book is .... (bad) than her others.
6 Some people think that the Sydney Opera House is .... (beautiful) modern building in the world.

GRAMMAR REFERENCE 83

who, which & where

The pronouns *who*, *which* and *where* can be used to add extra information to sentences. *Who* refers to people (and sometimes animals), *which* to things and *where* to places:

I've got a friend called Owen. He lives in Valencia.
*I've got a friend called Owen **who** lives in Valencia.*

I bought a jacket last week. It is really warm.
*I bought a jacket last week **which** is really warm.*

There's a really great phone shop in town. You can buy all the latest smartphones there.
*There's a really great phone shop in town **where** you can buy all the latest smartphones.*

Practice

4 Complete these sentences with *who*, *which* or *where*. Sometimes there may be more than one possible answer.

1. She doesn't like people .... are unfriendly.
2. That's the dog .... tried to bite me.
3. Where are the keys .... were on the kitchen table?
4. We're moving to a quiet place .... we can't hear the traffic.
5. The company .... David works for makes computers.

UNIT 4

Adjectives: -ing/-ed

- Many English adjectives which end in *-ing* or *-ed* are formed from verbs.

Verb	Adjectives
relax	relaxed / relaxing
surprise	surprised / surprising

- Adjectives which end in *-ed* tell us how a person feels:
*I'm going to bed because I'm **tired**.*

- Adjectives which end in *-ing* describe the effect:
*I'm going to bed. I've had a **tiring** day at work.*

Practice

1 Choose the correct adjectives.

1. **A:** Did you see that *interested / interesting* programme about the moon on TV last night?
   B: No, I'm not really *interested / interesting* in space.
2. **A:** You look very *relaxed / relaxing*. Did you have a good holiday?
   B: No, it wasn't *relaxed / relaxing* at all! I was ill the whole time.
3. **A:** What do you find most *annoyed / annoying* about your older brother?
   B: Everything he does makes me *annoyed / annoying*.
4. **A:** What's happened? You look really *excited / exciting*.
   B: Yes, I've just heard that I've won first prize in a competition. It's so *excited / exciting*!

Present perfect

We use the present perfect to connect the present with the past.

Positive/Negative forms		
I/You/We/They	have/'ve have not / haven't	finished work.
He/She/It	has/'s has not / hasn't	

Question forms & short answers		
Have	I/you/we/they	finished work?
Has	he/she/it	
Yes,	I/you/we/they	have.
	he/she/it	has.
No,	I/you/we/they	haven't.
	he/she/it	hasn't.

The present perfect is formed with the correct present form of *have* and the past participle of the main verb. The past participle of regular verbs and some irregular verbs is the same as the past simple. The past participle is underlined in the examples below.

Past simple	Present perfect
I **finished** work.	I **have finished** work.
He **bought** a sandwich.	He **has bought** a sandwich.

- Some irregular verbs have past participles which are not the same as the past simple form.

Past simple	Present perfect
She **ate** her lunch.	She **has eaten** her lunch.
She **wrote** a letter.	She **has written** a letter.

We use the present perfect to talk about:
- something which started in the past and is connected with the present:
*Ed **has broken** his leg, so he can't play football this weekend.*
- something which started in the past and is still true:
*Ben and Karen **have lived** in London for seven years.*
- past experiences which refer to an unstated time in the past, often with *ever* and *never*:
*Anna **has been** to Brazil, but she **has never been** to Canada.*
- recent past actions:
***Have** you **done** your homework?*

84

ever, never, yet, already & just

- *ever* (= until now) is used in questions to ask about past experiences:
  Have you **ever stayed** up all night?
- *never* (= until now) is used instead of a negative to talk about past experiences:
  I **have never visited** China.
- *yet* (= until now) is used in negative sentences and questions to talk about things we plan to do in the future, but which are not done. *Yet* is placed at the end of a sentence:
  I **haven't finished** my project **yet**.
  Have you **finished** your project **yet**?
- *already* (= before now, often sooner than expected):
  He'**s already done** his homework, so he can go out.
- *just* (= very recently, a short time ago):
  I'**ve just texted** Marcus and told him the good news.

Already and *just* are placed between *have/has* and the past participle.

Practice

2 Complete these sentences with *already*, *just* or *yet*.

1 I've .... finished my homework. I finished it a minute ago.
2 **A:** Let's tell our friends the news.
  B: I've .... told them. I told them last week.
3 I'm not hungry because I've .... had lunch. I ate earlier.
4 Have you met Ben .... ?
5 I haven't got dressed .... because I've just woken up.

since & for

We can use *since* and *for* with the present perfect to talk about a time that started in the past and continues to the present.
- *since* is followed by the beginning of a period of time:
  We've lived here **since** December 2017.
- *for* is followed by a period of time:
  She's lived there **for** six and a half years.

Practice

3 Complete these sentences with *since* or *for*.

1 My father has worked for the same company .... 20 years.
2 Megan has played football .... she was six years old.
3 I haven't eaten anything .... seven o'clock this morning.
4 Sofia can't still be tired. She's slept .... 11 hours!
5 I've made lots of new friends .... I've been at this school.

The present perfect or the past simple?

- We use the present perfect to talk about a past experience without saying when it happened:
  I'**ve been** to the top of the Eiffel Tower.
- We use the past simple to say when something happened:
  I **went** to the top of the Eiffel Tower last summer.
- We use the present perfect to talk about the continuing effect of a past event or action on the present:
  There **has been** an accident on the motorway. Now there are long queues of traffic into the city centre.
- We use the present perfect to talk about the time period up to the present:
  I'**ve been** to town this morning. (= It is still the morning.)
  My brother **has written** a short story. (= He may write more stories.)
- If the time period is now over, we use the past simple:
  I **went** into town this morning. (= It is now afternoon or evening.)
  Prince **wrote** over 150 songs. (= He died in 2016, so he cannot write any more.)

Practice

4 Complete these conversations with the past simple or present perfect of the verbs in brackets. Make any other changes necessary.

1 **A:** You look terrible. Are you OK?
  B: I'm all right. I .... (go) to bed late last night and I .... (just wake up).
2 **A:** Where's Chloe?
  B: I don't know. Her train .... (arrive) half an hour ago, but I .... (not see her yet).
3 **A:** Shall we go and see the new Star Wars film tonight?
  B: No, I .... (already see) it.
  A: Really?
  B: Yes, I .... (see) it last week.
4 **A:** What's the most expensive thing you .... (ever buy)?
  B: My racing bike. It .... (cost) 500 euros.
  A: I .... (never spend) as much money as that on anything!
5 **A:** .... (you ever do) gymnastics?
  B: Yes, but I .... (never do) karate.
6 **A:** Where .... (you go) on holiday last year?
  B: We .... (go) to Florida.
  A: Really? I've got relatives in Orlando, but I .... (never visit) them.

GRAMMAR REFERENCE

5 Underline and correct the mistakes in five lines of this conversation.

A: Have you heard? My oldest sister's getting married.
B: Who to?
A: A guy called Elliot.
B: Really! How long *did she know* him?
A: Only six months. Apparently they've *met* at work.
B: Have you met Elliot *already*?
A: No, not yet, but my sister's told me a lot about him.
B: When was the last time you've *seen* her?
A: I've *seen* her last week. She drove me to school one day.

UNIT 5
Future forms

will

Positive/Negative forms		
I/You/He/She/It/We/They	**will/'ll**	be late home.
	will not / won't	

Question forms & short answers		
Will	I/you/he/she/it/we/they	be late home?
Yes,	I/you/he/she/it/we/they	**will**.
No,	I/you/he/she/it/we/they	**won't**.

We use *will* to talk about:
- things we expect to happen or things we predict will happen:
  More people **will** buy electric cars in the future.
- things which are not certain:
  It probably **won't** be cold tomorrow.
- future facts:
  My app says that the sun **will** rise at five o'clock tomorrow morning.
- quick decisions about what to do next:
  There's someone at the door. I**'ll** get it.
- an offer or a promise:
  Don't worry. I **won't** be late.

be going to

Positive/Negative forms		
I	**am/'m** **am not / 'm not**	going to study tonight.
You/We/They	**are/'re** **are not / aren't**	
He/She/It	**is/'s** **is not / isn't**	

Question forms & short answers		
Am	I	**going to** study hard?
Are	you/we/they	
Is	he/she/it	
Yes,	I	**am**.
	you/we/they	**are**.
	he/she/it	**is**.
No,	I	**am/'m not**.
	you/we/they	**aren't**.
	he/she/it	**isn't**.

We use *going to* to talk about …
- things we predict based on what we can see, or something that we think is certain to happen:
  I**'m going to** sneeze.
- future plans and things we intend to do:
  I**'m going to** watch the match on TV.

Present continuous for the future

We use the present continuous to talk about arrangements or plans which have already been made:
I**'m starting** a new course tomorrow.

Present simple for the future

We use the present simple to talk about …
- events in the future that are certain because they are facts:
  The sun **rises** at 6.50 tomorrow morning.
- fixed or planned events:
  The lesson **ends** at 7.30 this evening.

Practice

1 Choose the most appropriate option.

1 *We see / We're going to see* the new Spider-Man film tomorrow. I bought the tickets online.
2 I don't think *I'll be / I am* late home. The lesson usually finishes at three o'clock.
3 I've got an important exam tomorrow, so *I go / I'm going to go* to bed early this evening.
4 Our train *leaves / is leaving* at 10.45 a.m. tomorrow morning.
5 **A:** We've run out of bread.
   B: OK, *I'll go / I'm going to go* and get some more.

Modals (2)

could/couldn't

Could is similar to *can* because we use it to express ability, possibility and permission and to make requests and suggestions. However, we use *could* slightly differently:
- ability in the past:
  I **couldn't** understand what the teacher was asking us.
- hypothetical possibility:
  I think it **could** rain later.
- asking permission:
  Could I use your laptop? (*Can* is also possible here.)
- making requests:
  Could you help me with my homework? (*Can* is also possible here.)
- making suggestions:
  If it's a nice day, we **could** go to the beach. (*Can* is also possible here.)
  Note: Remember that for making suggestions / giving advice, we often use the modal verb *should*.

may & might

These modals express the idea that 'it is possible' and are very similar. However, in some situations only *may* is possible:
- hypothetical possibility:
  I think it **may/might** rain later. (*Could* is also possible here.)
- asking permission:
  May I go to the toilet? (*Could* and *can* are also possible here.)
- expressing permission:
  Students **may not** run inside the school building. (*Can't/cannot* are also possible here.)

Practice

2 Choose the most appropriate option. Sometimes more than one answer is possible.

1 Last night, the neighbours had a noisy party and I *can't / couldn't / may not* get to sleep until after midnight.
2 *May / Can / Could* I borrow your pen for a moment?
3 I think that England *may / might / could* win next World Cup.
4 If you need some money, you *could / should / can* get a part-time job.
5 Rocio isn't in class today either. She *can / could / might* still be ill.
6 My bicycle is broken. *May / Can / Could* you help me fix it?

UNIT 6

used to

	Positive/Negative forms	
I/You/He/She/It/We/They	used to	enjoy watching football.
	did not / didn't use to	

	Question forms & short answers		
Did	I/you/he/she/it/we/they	use to	play football?
Yes,	I/you/he/she/it/we/they	did.	
No,		didn't.	

We use *used to* to talk about the past. There is no present form of *used to*.
Note: In negative and question forms, the spelling is *use* not *used*.

We use *used to* + an infinitive form to talk about …
- things that happened regularly in the past but do not happen now:
  I **used to** drink milk for breakfast, but now I always drink orange juice.
- actions that did not happen in the past, but happen now:
  I **didn't use to** drink orange juice, but now I have three glasses a day.
- past states or conditions that are different now from in the past:
  I **used to** have long, dark hair. (= I don't any more.)

Practice

1 Rewrite these sentences using the correct form of *used to*.

1 I like hot weather now, but I didn't in the past.
   I didn't use to like hot weather.
2 My brother played football regularly until he broke his leg.
   ....
3 My hair was brown, now it's black.
   ....
4 When I was younger, I didn't get up late.
   ....
5 Did you go on holiday with your parents when you were a child?
   ....

GRAMMAR REFERENCE 87

Verbs followed by infinitive / -ing form

- Some verbs are always followed by an infinitive (*to* + verb):
  When I was 15, I **decided to become** a professional musician.
- Others are always followed by the *-ing* form of the verb:
  Mike **kept falling** asleep during the lesson.

- There are some verbs which can be followed by either an infinitive or the *-ing* form.
- Unfortunately, there are no rules to help you work out whether verbs are followed by the infinitive or the *-ing* form, or either, so you will need to learn them.

Verbs followed by the infinitive

| afford   agree   arrange   attempt   choose   decide   expect   help   hope   intend   learn   manage   offer   plan   promise   refuse   seem   want   would like |

Verbs followed by -ing

| admit   avoid   can't stand*   consider   dislike*   don't mind*   enjoy*   fancy*   feel like   finish   give up   imagine   mind   miss   postpone   practise   prevent   put off   suggest |

Note: The verbs marked * all express likes or dislikes and were covered in Unit 1.

Verbs followed by the infinitive or -ing with no difference in meaning

| begin   continue   intend   start |

Verbs followed by the infinitive or -ing with little difference in meaning

| hate   like   love   prefer |

- There is a small difference in meaning between the two forms:
  – *-ing* form: the action or experience is more important:
    He **likes baking** cakes.
  – infinitive form: the result of the action is more important, or it describes a habit / something we prefer:
    He **likes to bake** cakes for special occasions.
- The *-ing* form is more common after *hate* and *love*:
  I **hate playing** ball sports. I **love doing** gymnastics.

Verbs followed by the infinitive or -ing where there is a clear difference in meaning

	Infinitive	-ing
forget	I **forgot to say** thank you. (= I did not say thank you.)	I **forgot saying** that. (= I have no memory of this.)
go on	He **went on to talk** about his childhood. (= This was the next thing he talked about.)	He **went on talking**. (= He continued talking.)
remember	I **remembered to lock** the door. (= I did something I had to do.)	I **remember locking** the door. (= I have a memory of this.)
stop	Let's **stop to buy** flowers. (= in order to do something)	Let's **stop buying** flowers. (= not continue)
try	I **tried to learn** Japanese, but it was too difficult, so I stopped. (= try something, and not succeed)	I **tried eating** spinach, but I didn't like it. (= try something and find out what it is like)

- In negative sentences, we can put *not* after the first verb:
  He's **decided not to go** to university next year.
  She **considered not going** away for the weekend. (= but now she is going)
- In sentences which include an object, we put the object after the first verb:
  I **helped my friend to do** his homework.
  We should **stop people using** their phones while they're driving.

Practice

2 Complete this conversation with the correct form of the verbs in brackets.

A: It's really hot here, isn't it? Do you fancy
   (1) .... (go) for a swim?
B: Yes, I'd love **(2)** .... (have) a swim.
A: Can I suggest **(3)** .... (go) this afternoon?
B: I'd planned **(4)** .... (go) to the cinema this afternoon, but I don't mind **(5)** .... (do) that tomorrow instead.
A: I can't imagine **(6)** .... (live) in a hot country all the time.
B: I'm sure you'd manage **(7)** .... (have) a nice time.
A: Maybe I'd get used to it. I certainly enjoy
   (8) .... (spend) my summer holidays here.

3 Tick (✓) the pairs of sentences which have the same meanings.

1. **A:** The teacher continued to talk even though the bell had rung for the end of class.
   B: The teacher continued talking even though the bell had rung for the end of class. ☐
2. **A:** I began to learn German two years ago.
   B: I began learning German two years ago. ☐
3. **A:** Ben stopped to phone his parents.
   B: Ben stopped phoning his parents. ☐
4. **A:** I prefer to watch football than to play it.
   B: I prefer watching football than playing it. ☐
5. **A:** I like to watch the sunrise.
   B: I like watching the sunrise. ☐
6. **A:** They went on to tell us about their holiday.
   B: They went on telling us about their holiday. ☐

do, make, have, go

Do, *make*, *have* and *go* are often confused in special phrases.

- *Do* is used to talk about work, jobs and activities: *do well, do badly, do the shopping, do an exercise, do your homework, do research, do the ironing, do a puzzle, do your best, do someone a favour, do the washing-up*:
  You must **do your homework** tonight.
  Can you **do the shopping** later?
- *Make* is generally used to talk about creating or producing something: *make a meal, make lunch, make some coffee*.
  It is also used in many phrases, e.g. *make your bed, make a choice, make friends, make a mistake, make a phone call, make up your mind, make a mess, make progress, make (a) noise*:
  I haven't **made up my mind** yet whether I'm going to tell her or not.
  The children **made a terrible mess** in their bedroom.
- *Have* is often used in phrases where some other languages use the equivalent of *do* instead, e.g. *have breakfast, have lunch, have dinner, have a shower, have a bath, have a drink, have an argument, have a party, have a break, have a chat*:
  What time do you **have breakfast**?
  I used to **have a bath** every day, but now I **have a shower** instead.
- *Go* is often used with gerunds (the *-ing* form of the verb which is used like a noun), e.g. *go swimming, go camping, go shopping*.
  It is also used in many phrases, e.g. *go to bed, go home, go to school, go well/badly, go wrong, go for a walk*:
  I **go to bed** early on weekdays, but later at the weekend.
  I made a cake, but it **went wrong** and tasted awful!

Practice

4 Complete these sentences with the correct form of *do, make, have* or *go*.

1. Learning Chinese is very difficult, but I'm .... progress.
2. Sam studied hard for the test, but it didn't .... well at all.
3. Anna and Natasha .... an argument yesterday and now they're not talking to each other.
4. .... the exercise on page 20.
5. Would you please stop .... so much noise? I'm trying to sleep.
6. Do you fancy .... lunch with me at the new pizza restaurant in town?

UNIT 7

Past perfect

Positive/Negative forms		
I/You/He/She/It/We/They	**had/'d**	**finished** school by five o'clock.
	had not / hadn't	

Question forms & short answers		
Had	I/you/he/she/it/we/they	**finished** school by five o'clock?
Yes,	I/you/he/she/it/we/they	**had**.
No,	I/you/he/she/it/we/they	**hadn't**.

We use the past perfect to …

- make clear the order of past events. The past perfect describes something that happened before another action/event in the past:
  My parents **had left** when I arrived home. (= My parents were not there when I arrived home.)
- say what was completed before a specific past time:
  By nine o'clock, I**'d phoned** three people and **had sent** five emails.
- explain past events or situations or give background information:
  I**'d got** up at five o'clock, so by midday I was very tired.
  She**'d drunk** nothing all day, so she was really thirsty.
- talk about situations that have changed:
  I**'d planned** to finish writing my essay this morning, but I've got a terrible headache.

Practice

1 Complete these sentences with the past simple or past perfect of the verbs in brackets.

1. It .... (rain) all night and, although it .... (stop), the ground .... (be) still very wet.
2. We .... (plan) to have a picnic, but then it started raining, so we .... (have to) think of something else to do.
3. It .... (be) sunny every day for two weeks, but then it .... (start) to snow.
4. We .... (cannot) go for a walk in the forest yesterday because the snow and ice .... (make) the paths too dangerous.
5. Yesterday, we .... (go) to the cinema because there was a new film that none of us .... (see).

Reported speech

- Direct speech is what we call the words people actually say when they speak. In the example below, the direct speech is underlined:
  He said, '<u>I haven't seen you for a long time.</u>'
- Indirect speech (also called reported speech) is how we report (tell) what another person says:
  He said he hadn't seen me for a long time.
- Tenses often change when we report what people said.

Direct speech	Reported speech
present simple 'I **go** to a school in the city centre.'	past simple She said she **went** to a school in the city centre.
present continuous 'I**'m waiting** for a bus.'	past continuous He said he **was waiting** for a bus.
present perfect 'I **have** already **had** lunch.'	past perfect He said he **had** already **had** lunch.
past simple 'I **enjoyed** my dinner.'	past perfect She said she **had enjoyed** her dinner.
will future 'I**'ll** call you later.'	would She said she **would** call me later.
can 'I **can** speak four languages.'	could He said he **could** speak four languages.
must 'You **must** be home by 10 p.m.'	had to She said he **had to** be home by 10 p.m.

- There is no change to reported speech with the past perfect and the modals *would, could, should, might* and *ought to*:
  'I hadn't eaten sushi before.' → She said she hadn't eaten sushi before.
  'You should visit the new zoo.' → He said I should visit the new zoo.

- We also need to make other changes when we report what people said.
  - Subject and object pronouns:
    'I have already told **you**.' → She said she had already told **me**.
    '**We** live in Paris.' → **They** said **they** lived in Paris.
  - Possessive adjectives:
    'I've mended **my** bike.' → He said he'd mended **his** bike.
    'We love **our** new flat.' → They said they loved **their** new flat.
  - Time references:
    'We're going on holiday **tomorrow**.' → They said they were going on holiday **the next day**.
    'I'll see you **next week**.' → She said she'd see me **the following week**.
  - Place references:
    'I want to stay **here**.' → He said he wanted to stay **there**.

Say & *tell* in reported speech

- We use *say* if we do not mention the person who is being spoken to:
  He **said** he was going to the theatre.
- We always use *tell* with a direct object (the person or thing that is affected by the action of the verb):
  She **told me** she was Russian.

Reported commands

We can use *tell* to report commands. We need to include the object (the person who needs to listen to the command) + infinitive after *tell*.

Direct commands	Reported commands
'Stop talking!' 'Don't be late!'	The teacher **told them to stop** talking. The father **told his daughter not to be** late.

Practice

2 Write this reported speech as direct speech.

1. She said she was living in Moscow.
   'I'm living in Moscow.'
2. I said I was sorry, but I couldn't lend her any more money.
   ....
3. He says he still feels ill.
   ....
4. She says she's older than me.
   ....
5. They said they'd come and see me later.
   ....
6. Max said he'd left the day before.
   ....
7. She told him to stop worrying.
   ....

3 Write these statements and commands as reported speech.

1 'I'm leaving school at the end of next year.'
He said ....
2 'I've got a surprise for you.'
She said ....
3 'Shut the door!'
She told him ....
4 'We've all passed our English exam.'
They said ....
5 'It's my birthday tomorrow.'
He said ....
6 'You're the only person I know who likes classical music.'
She said ....
7 'Don't drink any more coffee!'
He told Max ....
8 'We went to Morocco for our holiday last year.'
They said ....

Reported questions

The word order in reported questions is the same as for positive phrases.

Positive phrase	Direct question	Reported question
I **was smiling**.	'Why are you smiling?'	He asked me why I **was smiling**.

We use *ask* when we report questions. We need to make changes to tenses, pronouns, times and places. We do not use question marks.

Direct question	Reported question
'Why are you smiling?'	He **asked** me why I was smiling.
'What are you doing **tomorrow**?'	She asked us what we were doing **the next day**.
'When do **you** finish football practice?'	He asked **me** when I finished football practice.
'Why did you come **here**?'	She asked me why I had gone **there**.

With *yes/no* questions (questions that need either a *yes* or *no* answer), we need to use *if* or *whether* after *ask*.

Direct question	Reported question
'**Are** you feeling OK?'	She asked **if/whether** I was feeling OK.
'**Do** you need a break?'	He asked **if/whether** I needed a break.

Practice

4 Rewrite these indirect sentences as direct questions.

1 They asked me why I was there.
'Why are you here?'
2 Helen asked me if I was enjoying my new course.
....
3 Alex asked if anyone had found his keys.
....
4 Sasha wanted to know what we'd done the day before.
....
5 I asked Veronika if she could come to my party that evening.
....
6 We asked a policeman if he could tell us where the station was.
....
7 Jan wanted to know who my favourite actor was.
....
8 I asked my brother if he had tried to phone me.
....

5 Rewrite these questions as reported questions.

1. 'Why are you wearing your best clothes?'
   My mum asked ....
2. 'Where are you going?'
   My dad asked ....
3. 'What are you going to do there?'
   My brother asked ....
4. 'Are you going with anyone?'
   My sister asked ....
5. 'Do I know who you're going with?'
   My dad asked ....
6. 'What time will you be back?'
   My mum asked ....
7. 'How will you get home?'
   My brother asked ....
8. 'What will you do if you miss the last bus?'
   My sister asked ....

The passive: present & past

- We form the passive with the correct form of *be* followed by the past participle.

Active	Passive
We feed our cat twice a day.	Our cat is fed twice a day.
They built our school in 2012.	Our school was built in 2012.

- We use passive verbs rather than active verbs when:
  – we are more interested in who or what is affected by the action of the verb than who or what does the action:
  *My car **was made** in France.* (The focus is on my car rather than the workers or the company that made it.)
  *We **were given** a lot of homework to do in the holidays.* (Here, we are the focus, not the homework or the teachers who gave the homework.)
  – we do not know who did the action:
  *My bike **was stolen** yesterday.* (I don't know who stole it.)
  – who or what did something is obvious:
  *The driver of the car **was arrested**.* (We know that the police arrest people, so we do not need to mention them.)
- To say who or what did the action in a passive sentence, we can add a *by* phrase:
  *This opera **was composed by** Mozart.* (Mozart is the person who did the action.)

Practice

6 Complete these sentences with the passive form of the verbs in brackets. Use the present simple or the past simple.

1. Last year's final, which .... (play) in the new stadium, ... (watch) by over two million people.
2. In the past, most children walked to school, but now many .... (take) by their parents. Most of them .... (drive) by car.
3. I've just finished reading a science-fiction novel that .... (write) in 1980. Many of the things that .... (predict) by the author have come true.

7 Change these active sentences into passive ones. Mention who did the action if necessary.

1. A vet sees our cat twice a year.
   ....
2. Last night, the police closed the roads because of the accident.
   ....
3. A famous author wrote the book.
   ....
4. They play cricket in Australia.
   ....
5. My father taught me how to sing.
   ....

UNIT 8

First & second conditional

We use conditional sentences to talk about possible situations or actions and their results. Conditional sentences usually have two clauses: a conditional (*if*) clause and a main clause (usually a result).

Possible situation or action (conditional clause)	Result (main clause)
If I see Matt,	I'll tell him to call you.

First conditional

- We use the first conditional to talk about likely situations/actions.

Conditional clause: *if* + present simple	Main clause: *will* + infinitive
If we go by bus,	we'll get there on time.
If we win the basketball match this afternoon,	we'll be so happy.

- We can also use modal verbs with future meaning (*shall, should, would, can, could, may, might*):
  If we collect enough money, we can buy our teacher a good present.

Second conditional

- We use the second conditional to talk about unlikely situations/actions. We can also use it to imagine situations in the present or future.

Conditional clause: *if* + past simple	Main clause: *would* + infinitive
If we went by bike,	*we'd get there very late.*
If I had a lot of money,	*I'd buy a new smartphone.*

- We can also use modal verbs with future-in-the-past meaning (*should, might, could*):
  If I knew how to snowboard, I could enter the competition.

- We can use *were* instead of *was* in the conditional clause:
  *If I **were/was** you, I'd look for a new hobby.*
  *If my sister **were/was** a nurse, all her patients would love her.*

Note: Conditional (*if*) clauses can come before or after the main clause in the first and second conditional.

I'll tell Matt to call you	*if I see him.*
If I see Matt,	*I'll tell him to call you.*
We'd go for a bike ride	*if it was sunny.*
If it was sunny,	*we'd go for a bike ride.*

- When the conditional clause comes before the main clause, it is followed by a comma:
  If I see Matt, I'll tell him to call you.

Practice

1 Match the sentence beginnings (1–8) with the correct endings (a–h) to make first and second conditional sentences.

1. If I have time,
2. If I had more time,
3. If you were nicer,
4. You wouldn't be tired in class
5. She would be really angry
6. If he phoned her,
7. If my computer breaks down again,
8. If I had enough money,

a. he'd invite you to his party.
b. she'd refuse to speak to him.
c. if she knew the truth.
d. I'll phone you.
e. I'll have to get a new one.
f. I'd buy a new computer.
g. I'd cycle to college every morning.
h. if you went to bed earlier.

2 Write second conditional sentences.

1. I'd like to do the high jump but I'm not very tall.
   If I were/was taller, I'd do the high jump.
2. She can't study in Canada because she doesn't speak English.
   If ....
3. I haven't got enough free time to learn to play a musical instrument.
   If ....
4. My uncle's too unfit to be a firefighter.
   If ....
5. I'd like to buy a laptop, but I haven't got enough money.
   If ....

Writing bank

MAKING YOUR WRITING MORE INTERESTING

To make a sentence more interesting, we can add more details.

1 Look at how the second sentence adds information (the underlined text). Match the new information (1–8) with the descriptions (a–h).

- *I went to Spain.*
  ¹Last year, I went to Spain, ²which is my favourite country.
- *I like warm weather.*
  I like warm weather, ³but I don't like cold weather.
- *My bike was broken.*
  My ⁴new bike was broken, ⁵so I had to walk to school.
- *George was happy.*
  George was ⁶really happy ⁷because it was his birthday.
- *I read the letter.*
  I read the letter ⁸slowly and carefully.

a adding a contrasting idea …… 3 ……
b giving a reason ………….
c saying when something happened …………….
d giving the result of an action …………….
e using a relative clause to give extra information …………….
f using an adjective to describe something …………….
g using an adverb to make an adjective stronger …………….
h using adverbs to describe how something happens …………….

2 Complete the table below with the words in the box.

> and   beautiful   because   but   completely   delicious
> easily   later that day   loudly   modern   quickly   so
> the next day   this morning   wonderful   yesterday

Adjectives	Adverbs	Linking words	Time expressions

3 Make these sentences more interesting. Use the words in the box. Can you think of any other words to use?

> but   early the next morning
> large   really   suddenly

1 It ………………. started to rain.
2 I called Max, ………………. he didn't answer his phone.
3 We set out for London ……………….
4 I ordered a cup of coffee and a ………………. slice of cake.
5 The film was ………………. boring!

4 Join the two parts of these sentences with *and*, *but*, *so* or *because*.

> we didn't play tennis – the weather was bad
>
> *We didn't play tennis because the weather was bad.*

1 I was very tired – I went straight to bed
   …………………………………………………
   …………………………………………………
2 we all went to the party – everyone had a great time
   …………………………………………………
   …………………………………………………
3 Paul wanted to come with us – he couldn't
   …………………………………………………
   …………………………………………………
4 we all laughed – it was so funny
   …………………………………………………
   …………………………………………………

WRITING PART 1: AN EMAIL

1 Read the exam task. What information should you include in the email?

Read this email from your English-speaking friend Sam, and the notes you have made.

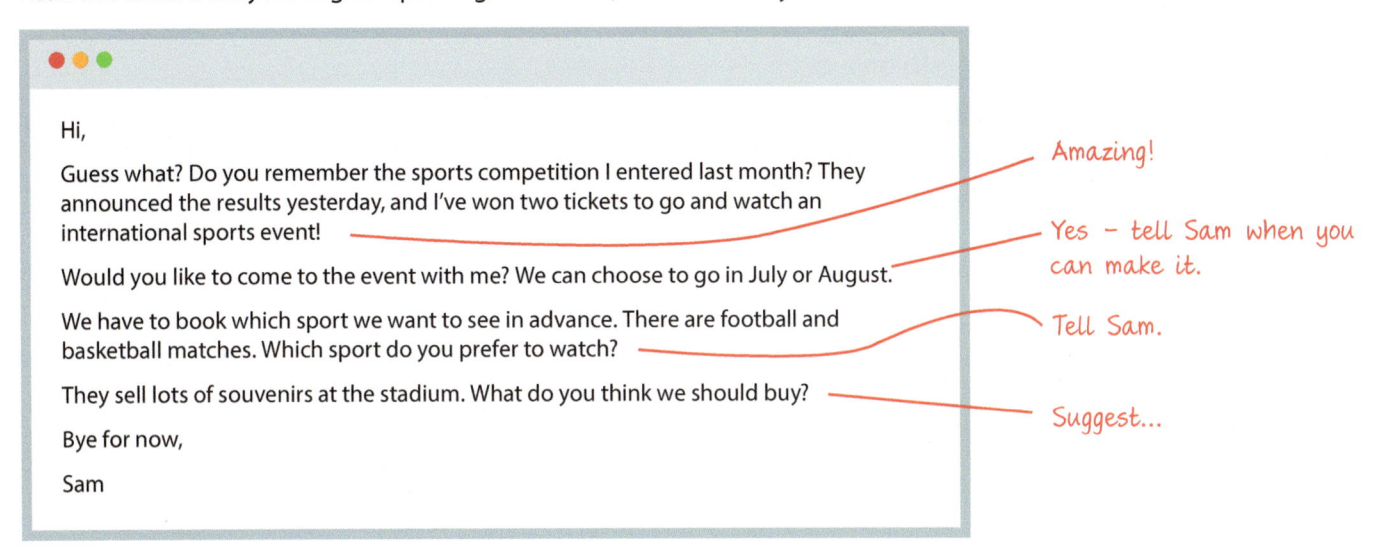

Hi,

Guess what? Do you remember the sports competition I entered last month? They announced the results yesterday, and I've won two tickets to go and watch an international sports event! — *Amazing!*

Would you like to come to the event with me? We can choose to go in July or August. — *Yes – tell Sam when you can make it.*

We have to book which sport we want to see in advance. There are football and basketball matches. Which sport do you prefer to watch? — *Tell Sam.*

They sell lots of souvenirs at the stadium. What do you think we should buy? — *Suggest...*

Bye for now,

Sam

Write your **email** to Sam, using **all** the **notes**.

MODEL ANSWER

Use an informal phrase to start the email.

Hi, Sam

Thanks for your email. That's amazing news about the competition! Well done!

Yes, I love sport, so it would be incredible to go to a big sports event with you. I can go with you in July, but I can't go in August because I'm on holiday then.

I'm a big football fan, so I'd love to see an international football match. It would be brilliant to see some of my favourite heroes in action.

Why don't we buy football shirts as souvenirs? We can wear them at the match!

See you soon,

Tom

Remember you are replying to Sam's email.

This answers the question about when you can or can't make it, and gives a reason.

This answers the question 'Which sport do you prefer to watch?'

This is a suggestion.

Use an informal phrase at the end.

KEY LANGUAGE AND IDEAS FOR EMAILS

Opening an email
Hi   Hi, Tom   Hi, there   Hello

Closing an email
Love,   See you soon,   Take care,   Bye

Responding to an email
Thanks for your email.   It's good to hear from you.

Responding to good news
That's amazing news!   I'm so happy for you!   Wow!   How exciting!
Well done!

Responding to bad news
I'm sorry to hear about …

Making a suggestion
Why don't you/we … ?   You/We could …   If I were you, I'd …
Make sure you …

Making an offer or promise
I could … if you like.   Would you like me to … ?   I can … if you want.

Making a request
Could you … ?   Can you … ?   Would you mind … -ing?

Giving good or bad news
You'll be pleased to hear that …   I'm afraid …
Guess (who/what/where/how/etc.) … !   I'm sorry, but …

Linking words and phrases
and   but   so   because   also   as well

Informal language
- contractions: I'm   you're   he's
- informal words and phrases: awesome   great   keep in touch   take care
I guess …
- exclamation marks to show emotion: That's great news!   Wow!

2 Match the beginnings and endings of these sentences. Then decide if each sentence is a suggestion (S), an offer (O), a promise (P) or a request (R).

1 Could you   a I'd definitely accept the job. …………
2 If I were you,   b some useful addresses if you want. …………
3 I can send you   c be there to help on the day. …………
4 Don't worry, I'll   d let me know what time you're arriving? …………

3 Correct the underlined mistakes in these sentences giving good or bad news.
Use the Key language and ideas box above to check your answers.

1 <u>I afraid</u> I won't be able to come to your party.
2 <u>Guess that where</u> I'm going next week?
3 I'm sorry, <u>and</u> Dan won't be here when you visit.
4 <u>You'll be pleased hear</u> that I've now finished all my exams!

4 Choose the correct linking words.

1 I finish work at six o'clock, *because / so* I can meet you at 6.30.
2 My sister Martha is *also / as well* coming home for the holidays.
3 I'm not very good at singing, *because / but* I still enjoy it.
4 I'm a bit disappointed *because / so* my exam results weren't brilliant.
5 I'll find the document *also / and* send it to you in an email.

5 Read the exam task. What information should you include in the email?

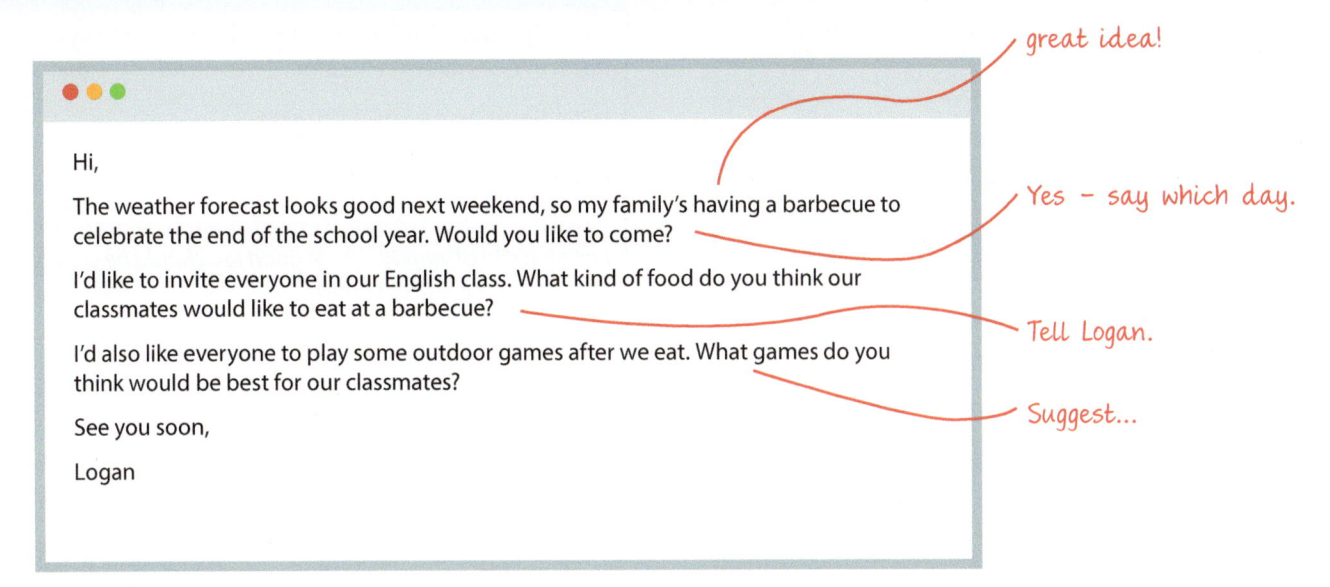

> Hi,
>
> The weather forecast looks good next weekend, so my family's having a barbecue to celebrate the end of the school year. Would you like to come?
>
> I'd like to invite everyone in our English class. What kind of food do you think our classmates would like to eat at a barbecue?
>
> I'd also like everyone to play some outdoor games after we eat. What games do you think would be best for our classmates?
>
> See you soon,
>
> Logan

- great idea!
- Yes – say which day.
- Tell Logan.
- Suggest...

6 Before you write your email, complete this table with ideas.

Paragraph 1 (respond to the invitation)	
Paragraph 2 (suggest some food)	
Paragraph 3 (explain your idea for a game)	
Useful phrases I can use	

7 Write your email, using your notes from Exercise 6. Write about 100 words.

8 Check your email and make changes if necessary.
- [ ] Have you answered all the questions and included all the necessary information?
- [ ] Have you used a suitable phrase to open and close your email?
- [ ] Have you tried to make your writing more interesting by adding details?
- [ ] Have you used informal language?
- [ ] Have you used linking words and phrases?
- [ ] Have you counted your words?

WRITING BANK

WRITING PART 2: AN ARTICLE

1 Read this exam task. What should your article be about? What information should it include?

> **Articles wanted!**
>
> **My favourite city**
>
> What's your favourite city?
>
> What's so special about this city?
>
> What city would you love to travel to in the future?
>
> Tell us what you think!
>
> Write an article answering these questions and we will publish the most interesting ones on our website.

MODEL ANSWER

My favourite city is Paris because it is so lively and interesting. It is also full of surprises.

Paris is a city of variety. It has many beautiful old buildings, but it also feels modern. You can visit expensive designer shops or small, traditional markets. There are hundreds of restaurants which serve French food, or different food from around the world. You can meet all kinds of people, too. There is something for everyone.

I would love to travel to New York in the future because I've seen the city in so many films, and I would love to visit it in real life.

The first paragraph answers the first question and gives a reason.

Adjectives make the article more interesting to read.

The second paragraph gives more details and answers the second question in the task.

The third paragraph is about a city the writer would like to go to in the future.

KEY LANGUAGE AND IDEAS FOR ARTICLES

Use adjectives for describing people and things
attractive   brave   calm   cheerful   convenient

Use linking words and phrases
and   but   so   because   although   also   as well

Use an introductory sentence for each paragraph
Paris is a city of variety.   A good job should be creative.
Photography is a great hobby.

Give your opinion
I think …   It seems to me that …   I would say that …

2 Match the titles (1–6) with the article topics (a–f).
1 Me and my dog   a a restaurant
2 Work or pleasure?   b a holiday destination
3 A home of my own   c a favourite pet
4 Music to get you dancing d a good place to live
5 Full of flavour   e an enjoyable job
6 A place to relax   f a band or singer

3 Choose the best introductory sentence for each opening paragraph.

1 *There are many benefits to keeping fit. / I don't really do enough exercise.* Doing regular exercise is good for your heart, and it helps you to lose weight. It can also improve your mood, especially if you're feeling tired or unhappy.

2 *Some older people are not used to the internet. / The internet has changed people's lives in many ways.* People can now go online to do their shopping and book restaurants and holidays. Students also have access to lots of information that was difficult to find before the internet.

3 *Teaching is a very difficult job. / I would like to become a teacher.* Students are not always interested in learning, and teachers have to work hard to encourage their students to study. Also, there are sometimes problems with bad behaviour from students.

4 Complete the table below with the adjectives in the box. Can you add any more?

> amusing   delicious   freezing   frightening
> old-fashioned   peaceful   quiet   stormy   tasty   tight

Clothes	Films	Food	Countryside	Weather

5 Read this exam task. What should your article be about? What information should it include?

> **Articles wanted!**
>
> **My perfect job**
>
> What makes the perfect job?
>
> Is it being creative, travelling, meeting people, or something else?
>
> How important is it to earn a lot of money?
>
> Tell us what you think!
>
> **Write an article answering these questions and we will publish the most interesting articles on our website.**

6 Before you write your article, complete this table with ideas.

Paragraph 1 (answer the first question)	
Paragraph 2 (give more details)	
Paragraph 3 (give your opinion about money)	
Useful phrases I can use	

7 Write your article, using your notes from Exercise 6. Write about 100 words.

8 Check your article and make changes if necessary.
- [ ] Have you answered all the questions and included all the necessary information?
- [ ] Have you used adjectives to make your article interesting to read?
- [ ] Have you expressed a personal opinion?
- [ ] Have you used linking words and phrases?
- [ ] Have you counted your words?

WRITING BANK

WRITING PART 2: A STORY

1 Read this exam task. Which is the best way to continue the story (1, 2 or 3)? Why?

> Your English teacher has asked you to write a story.
> Your story must begin with this sentence:
> *I opened the letter from my cousins in Brazil.*
> Write your **story** in about **100** words.

1. I have three cousins who live in Brazil, and I get on very well with them. They are all very keen on football.
2. They said they were coming to visit me, and they were arriving on the 15th – today!
3. I think Brazil is a really interesting country, and I would love to go there one day. There are lots of amazing wild animals there.

MODEL ANSWER

> I opened the letter from my cousins in Brazil. They said they were coming to visit me, and they were arriving on the 15th – today! I was really excited. First, I cleaned everything in the flat. Then I went to the supermarket to buy food. After that, I made a cake to make them feel welcome. By evening, I was completely exhausted.
> I picked up the letter again to check the time of their flight, and that's when I noticed the date. They were arriving on July 15th, but today was June 15th!
> We had a wonderful time together in July, and all laughed about the mistake I had made!

- The first paragraph gives background to the story.
- The second paragraph gives the main events of the story.
- Time expressions make the order of events clear.
- Adjectives and adverbs make the story more interesting.
- The last paragraph ends the story.

KEY LANGUAGE AND IDEAS FOR STORIES

Use past simple verbs for the main events
I went to a restaurant.   I found a letter.

Use past continuous verbs for longer actions in the past
I was waiting for the bus.   The sun was shining.

Use past perfect verbs for background events
Unfortunately, I had forgotten my purse.

Time expressions
first   then   later   the next day   finally

Adjectives to describe people
friendly   kind   tall

Adjectives to describe places
busy   quiet   modern

Adjectives to describe feelings
excited   angry   delighted

Adverbs to describe how someone does something
quickly   slowly   carefully

Adverbs to comment on what happened
luckily   fortunately   unfortunately

2 Complete these sentences with the correct form of the verbs in brackets. Use the past simple, past continuous or past perfect.

1. I packed my bags and then .... (call) a taxi to take me to the airport.
2. Sara .... (wait) for me when I got to the restaurant.
3. I could finally relax because I .... (pass) all my exams!
4. I found an old key while I .... (walk) along the beach.
5. James was late because he .... (forget) to set his alarm.
6. I opened the door and then quickly .... (close) it again.

3 Choose the correct time expressions.

I was really scared when my car broke down near the forest. (**1**) *Then / First*, I tried starting the car, but that didn't work. (**2**) *Finally / Then*, I tried to call a friend, but I had no signal on my phone. (**3**) *Next / After*, I decided to wait for another car so I could ask for help. (**4**) *An hour later / Before an hour*, I was still sitting there! Suddenly, I heard the sound of another car. (**5**) *Finally / After*, someone came to help me and I got home safely.

4 Complete the sentences below with adjectives in the box.

> curly   disappointed   entertaining   messy
> smart   spicy

1. The room was .... and not very clean.
2. She was wearing a very nice .... jacket and skirt.
3. He cooked some delicious, ... food for us.
4. The show was fun and very ....
5. She introduced me to a tall young man with .... hair.
6. I was very .... when she didn't call me.

5 Read this exam task. Before you write your story, complete the table with ideas.

> Your English teacher has asked you to write a story. Your story must begin with this sentence:
> *Our day at the zoo began quite well.*
> Write your **story** in about **100** words.

Paragraph 1 (the background to the story)

Paragraph 2 (the main events)

Paragraph 3 (the ending)

Language I can use

6 Write your story, using your notes from Exercise 5.

7 Check your story and make changes if necessary.

- ☐ Does your story have a clear beginning, middle and ending?
- ☐ Have you used verbs in the past simple, past continuous and past perfect?
- ☐ Have you used time expressions to order the events?
- ☐ Have you used adjectives and adverbs to make your story interesting?
- ☐ Have you counted your words?

WRITING BANK

Speaking bank

SPEAKING PART 1

1 🔊 **37** Listen to Maria answering these questions. Does she use full sentences in her answers?

1. What's your name?
2. What's your surname?
3. Where do you come from?
4. Do you work, or are you a student?

2 🔊 **38** Listen to Maria answering more questions. Notice how she adds extra information.

1. What did you do yesterday evening?
2. Do you think that English will be useful to you in the future?
3. Tell us about a place you would like to visit in the future.
4. Can you describe your house or flat?
5. What do you enjoy doing in your free time?

KEY LANGUAGE AND IDEAS FOR PERSONAL QUESTIONS

Use frequency adverbs to talk about habits and routines
I usually have breakfast …
I often watch TV …

Use the past simple and time expressions to talk about the past
Yesterday, I watched …
Last weekend, I visited …

Use *be going to* and time expressions to talk about future plans
Next summer, I'm going to travel to …

Talk about future hopes
I'd like to visit …
I want to get a job …
I hope I'll work …

Add extra information
actually   and   also

Add contrasting information
but

Add reasons and results
because   so   that's why

Add examples
for example, …   for instance, …

3 🔊 38 Complete Maria's answers with the words/phrases in the box. Then listen again and check.

> actually   also   and   because   but   for example   often   so

1 I .... watch films with my friends.
2 I hope I'll travel to different countries with my job, ... I'm sure I will need English.
3 I'd love to go to New York one day .... it looks like such an exciting city.
4 .... , my uncle lives there.
5 The kitchen is very small, ... the living room is quite big.
6 .... , it's got a balcony.
7 I'm quite into sport, ... I do quite a lot of sport in my free time.
8 .... , I sometimes go running in the evenings.

4 Complete the table below with the time expressions in the box, according to whether they refer to the present, the past or the future.

> always   last night   last weekend   next weekend
> sometimes   tomorrow   tonight   usually
> when I was younger

Present simple	Past simple	*be going to*

SPEAKING BANK   103

5 🔊 39 **Match the questions (1–5) with the answers (a–e). Then choose one extra piece of information (f–j) to add to each answer. Then listen to Pablo and check.**

1 Tell us about your English teacher.
2 Would you like to live in a different country?
3 Can you tell us about your home town?
4 How do you usually travel to school or work?
5 What did you do last weekend?

a My home town is Barcelona. …
b His name's Mr Adams. …
c On Saturday, I played football. …
d I wouldn't like to for long. …
e I usually catch the bus. …

f It's on the coast.
g We usually have a match every Saturday.
h I'd miss my family and friends at home.
i He's really funny.
j I'd prefer to walk.

6 🔊 39 **How does Pablo introduce extra information? Complete these sentences. Then listen again and check.**

1 I like him .... he always makes our lessons interesting.
2 I'd like to visit different countries, ... the United States or maybe Australia.
3 There are lots of beautiful buildings .... are very famous.
4 I'd prefer to walk, ... it's too far for me.
5 We usually have a match every Saturday. ...., we didn't win last week.

7 Practise answering these questions. Use a range of tenses, and add extra information.

- What's your name?
- What's your surname?
- Where do you come from?
- Do you work, or are you a student?

- What did you do yesterday evening?
- Do you think that English will be useful to you in the future?
- Tell us about a place you would like to visit in the future.
- Can you describe your house or flat?

- What do you enjoy doing in your free time?
- Tell us about your English teacher.
- Would you like to live in a different country?
- Can you tell us about your home town?
- How do you usually travel to school or work?
- What did you do last weekend?

SPEAKING PART 2

1 🔊 40 Listen to Pablo describing a photo. What guesses does he make?

> **KEY LANGUAGE AND IDEAS FOR DESCRIBING A PHOTO**
>
> **Say what you can see**
> The photo shows …   I can see …   There's a …
> There are some …   but you can't see …   She's got …   He has …
>
> **Describe where things are in the photo**
> at the front   in the background   on the left   on the right   in the middle
> behind   in front of   next to
>
> **Use the present continuous**
> He's wearing …   She's running …
>
> **Talk about the people**
> tall   long/short hair   young   old
>
> **Talk about the place**
> indoors   outdoors   attractive   comfortable   safe
>
> **Talk about the weather**
> sunny   cloudy   wet
>
> **When you don't know the word for something**
> It's a kind of …   It looks like a …
>
> **Make guesses**
> He looks like …   He seems to be …   I guess he's probably …   I think maybe …
> It might be …

SPEAKING BANK

2 Look at this photo. Choose the correct words in the sentences below to describe where the people are.

1 There are two young women *at the front / in the background* of the photo.
2 There's an old man with a beard on the *right / left*.
3 There's a young couple on the *left / right*, further back in the bus.
4 You can see someone's legs *behind / next to* the old man, but you can't see their face clearly.
5 *In the background / At the front*, you can see a man standing up.

3 Look at the photo again. Complete these sentences with the present continuous of the verbs in brackets. Then listen and check.
1 The photo shows some people who .... (travel) by bus.
2 The two women at the front of the photo .... (smile).
3 One woman .... (show) the other one something on her phone.
4 The older man on the right .... (look) forwards. Maybe he .... (think) about where to get off the bus.
5 In the background, there's a man who .... (stand) up. He .... (talk) to someone.

4 Look at this photo. Then complete the sentences below with words in the box.

| guess | looks | might | probably | seem |

1 I think the people are .... father and son.
2 They .... be watching TV.
3 They're eating something from a box. It .... like pizza.
4 They .... to be quite relaxed.
5 I .... they're probably having a relaxing evening at home.

5 🔊 42 Look at the photo again. Practise describing it. Then listen and compare your ideas.

6 Practise describing the photos on this page and page 109.

SPEAKING BANK 109

SPEAKING PART 3

1 🔊 43 Listen to two students doing the task below. Do they talk about all the options? Which present do they agree on?

> It is your friend's birthday soon, and you would like to buy her a present. Here are some ideas.
> Talk together about the different presents you could buy, and say which would be the most suitable.

KEY LANGUAGE AND IDEAS FOR DISCUSSING OPTIONS

Making suggestions
What about … ?   What do you think about … ?   Would … be a good idea?

Responding to suggestions
That's a great idea.   Yes, good idea.   I'm not sure.

Giving your opinion
I think …   In my opinion, …

Asking someone's opinion
What do you think?   Do you agree?

Agreeing
That's true.   I agree (with you).   Yes, I think you're right.   OK, so …

Disagreeing
I don't agree with you because …   I'm not sure about that because …

Considering alternatives
… might be a better choice.   What if we … ?

Reaching agreement
It's time to decide.   Are you OK with that?   We'll go for that one, then.

2 🔊 43 **Complete the discussion below with words in the box. Then listen again and check.**

| agree | go | idea | OK | opinion | so | sure | think |

A: What do you (**1**) .... about that idea?
B: I'm not (**2**) .... It's difficult to choose a book for someone else.
A: I (**3**) .... with you. And I don't think flowers are a good idea, because they're a bit boring, in my (**4**) ....
B: Would a T-shirt be a good (**5**) .... ? Most people wear T-shirts.
A: Well, I don't really like it when people buy me clothes, because I prefer to choose them myself.
B: OK, (**6**) .... not a T-shirt … Maybe we should choose the cinema tickets. Are you (**7**) .... with that?
A: Yes, good idea. We'll (**8**) .... for that one, then.

3 **Match the beginnings and endings of these sentences.**

1 That's a
2 Do you
3 I don't
4 Flowers might
5 It's time
6 Yes, I think

a agree with you.
b be a better choice.
c to decide.
d great idea.
e you're right.
f agree?

4 🔊 44 **Work in pairs. Do the task below. Then listen and compare your ideas.**

Discuss how your class should celebrate the end of exams. Here are some ideas. Talk together about the different ideas and say which would be the most fun.

SPEAKING PART 4

1 🔊 45 Listen to two students answering the questions below. Which things in the box do they do?

- give reasons for their answers ☐
- interrupt each other ☐
- ask for each other's opinions ☐
- disagree with each other ☐
- use an expression to allow time to think about the answer ☐

1 Who do you most enjoy buying presents for?
2 Which people in your family are the most difficult to choose presents for?
3 Do you like receiving money instead of presents?

KEY LANGUAGE AND IDEAS FOR DISCUSSING IDEAS

Talking about likes/dislikes/preferences
I like/love + -ing   I prefer to …   I enjoy …

Talking about habits
I sometimes/usually/always …

Giving your opinion
I think …   In my opinion, …

Asking someone's opinion
What do you think?   Do you agree?

Agreeing
That's true.   I agree with you.
Yes, I think you're right.

Disagreeing
I don't agree with you because …
I'm not sure about that because …

Giving yourself time to think
That's an interesting question.
That's a difficult question.   Let me see.

2 Choose the correct words.

1 I enjoy *to buy / buying* things for my nephew.
2 It *sometimes is / is sometimes* nice to receive money.
3 I *usually get / get usually* money from three or four relatives.
4 I prefer *get / to get* money from people who don't know me very well.
5 I love *get / getting* presents.

3 Complete the dialogues below with the phrases in the box.

> Do you agree?
> That's an interesting question.
> That's true.
> What do you think?

1 **A:** I think surprise presents are the best presents.
   ....
   B: Yes, I do. I love opening presents when I have no idea what they are!
2 **A:** I think money is sometimes the most useful present to get.
   B: .... Because then you can use it to buy something you really need.
3 **A:** In my opinion, men are the most difficult people to buy presents for.
   ....
   B: Yes, I think you're right. I never know what to buy for my dad or my uncle.
4 **A:** Do you think that some people spend too much money on presents?
   B: Hmm. .... I think most people spend as much as they can afford.

4 Work in pairs. Discuss these questions.

> 1 Would you like to have more social events with your class?
> 2 Do you think watching sports events can be more fun than taking part?
> 3 Do you prefer cooking a meal for friends or eating out in a restaurant?

5 🔊 46 **Listen and compare your ideas.**

SPEAKING BANK 113

Irregular verbs

Verb	Past simple	Past participle
be	was / were	been
beat	beat	beaten
become	became	become
begin	began	begun
bend	bent	bent
bite	bit	bitten
bleed	bled	bled
blow	blew	blown
break	broke	broken
build	built	built
burn	burnt / burned	burnt / burned
buy	bought	bought
catch	caught	caught
choose	chose	chosen
come	came	come
cost	cost	cost
cut	cut	cut
deal	dealt	dealt
dig	dug	dug
do	did	done
draw	drew	drawn
dream	dreamt / dreamed	dreamt / dreamed
drink	drank	drunk
drive	drove	driven
eat	ate	eaten
fall	fell	fallen
feed	fed	fed
feel	felt	felt
fight	fought	fought
find	found	found
fly	flew	flown
forbid	forbade	forbidden
forget	forgot	forgotten
forgive	forgave	forgiven
freeze	froze	frozen
get	got	got
give	gave	given

Verb	Past simple	Past participle
go	went	gone
grow	grew	grown
hang	hung	hung
have	had	had
hear	heard	heard
hide	hid	hidden
hit	hit	hit
hold	held	held
hurt	hurt	hurt
keep	kept	kept
kneel	knelt	knelt
know	knew	known
lay	laid	laid
lead	led	led
learn	learnt / learned	learnt / learned
leave	left	left
lend	lent	lent
let	let	let
lie	lay	lain
lose	lost	lost
make	made	made
mean	meant	meant
meet	met	met
pay	paid	paid
put	put	put
read	read	read
ride	rode	ridden
ring	rang	rung
rise	rose	risen
run	ran	run
say	said	said
see	saw	seen
sell	sold	sold
send	sent	sent
set	set	set
sew	sewed	sewn
shake	shook	shaken
shine	shone	shone

Verb	Past simple	Past participle
shoot	shot	shot
show	showed	shown
shut	shut	shut
sing	sang	sung
sink	sank	sunk
sit	sat	sat
sleep	slept	slept
smell	smelt / smelled	smelt / smelled
speak	spoke	spoken
spell	spelt / spelled	spelt / spelled
spend	spent	spent
spill	spilt / spilled	spilt / spilled
spoil	spoilt / spoiled	spoilt / spoiled
stand	stood	stood
steal	stole	stolen
stick	stuck	stuck
strike	struck	struck
sweep	swept	swept
swim	swam	swum
swing	swung	swung
take	took	taken
teach	taught	taught
tear	tore	torn
tell	told	told
think	thought	thought
throw	threw	thrown
understand	understood	understood
wake	woke	woken
wear	wore	worn
win	won	won
write	wrote	written

Phrasal verb builder

A phrasal verb is a verb with two or three parts. The meaning of the verb is sometimes different from the meaning of its separate parts. Phrasal verbs can combine verbs with prepositions or adverbs.

This section focuses on phrasal verbs related to four topics: **relationships**, **travel**, **communication** and **daily routines**.

RELATIONSHIPS

1 Match the phrasal verbs in the box with the definitions below.

> look after someone   go out with someone
> bring up someone   split up with someone
> get together   get on with someone

1 .... = look after children until they are adults
2 .... = have a friendly relationship with someone
3 .... = meet
4 .... = have a romantic relationship with someone
5 .... = take care of someone
6 .... = end a relationship

2 Choose the correct option.

1 I *get on / get together* with my friends every weekend to play football.
2 I *split up / get on* with everyone in my family. Everyone's very friendly.
3 My grandparents *brought up / went out* four children in a very small house.
4 I need to *look after / bring up* my little sister when my parents go out.
5 The band *got together / split up* because they didn't enjoy playing together any more.

3 Write a sentence using each of the phrasal verbs.

TRAVEL

1 Match the phrasal verbs in the box with the definitions below.

> turn up   break down   check in   set off
> take off   get back

1 .... = when something (e.g. a car or computer) stops working
2 .... = arrive at an airport as a passenger, or a hotel as a guest
3 .... = return
4 .... = leave on a journey
5 .... = when a plane leaves the ground
6 .... = arrive, come

2 Complete these sentences with the past simple of the phrasal verbs in the box in Exercise 1.

1 We .... for the airport at seven o'clock in the morning.
2 After we had been driving for ten minutes, our car ...., so my dad called a garage. Five minutes later, a mechanic .... and fixed the problem.
3 When we got to the airport, we parked the car and .... at the departures desk.
4 Half an hour later, our plane ....and our holiday began!
5 When we ....home a week later, we felt very relaxed.

3 Write a sentence using each of the phrasal verbs.

116

COMMUNICATION

1 Match the phrasal verbs in the box with the definitions below.

> hang up   fill in something   call someone back
> switch something off   ring up someone

1 .... = return a phone call
2 .... = complete a form
3 .... = end a phone conversation
4 .... = make a phone call
5 .... = turn off something (e.g. computer)

2 Choose the correct options.

> My mobile phone stopped working yesterday, so I (**1**) *switched off / switched it off* and (**2**) *called back / rang up* a help line using my sister's phone. But the line was busy, so I (**3**) *filled in / hung up*. I waited ten minutes and then (**4**) *rang up / called back*. The person who answered the phone asked me to (**5**) *ring up / fill in* an online form, and gave me another number to call. In ten minutes, my mobile phone was working again!

3 Write a sentence using each of the phrasal verbs.

DAILY ROUTINES

1 Match the phrasal verbs in the box with the definitions below.

> tidy up   wake someone up   get up
> put something on   pick someone up

1 .... = get out of bed
2 .... = collect someone in a car
3 .... = put clothes on your body
4 .... = make a place look clean
5 .... = stop (someone) sleeping

2 Complete the paragraph below with the present simple of the phrasal verbs in the box in Exercise 1. Add any other words you need.

> I try to help at home, because my parents are really busy. I always (**1**) .... my room and help with my five-year-old brother, too. He has just started school. Every morning, I (**2**) .... at 7.00. At 7.15, he (**3**) .... and (**4**) .... his school clothes. Then he watches TV while he is having breakfast. At 8.00, his friend's mum (**5**) .... in her car and takes him to school.

3 Write a sentence using each of the phrasal verbs.

PHRASAL VERB BUILDER

Wordlist

adj = adjective, *adv* = adverb, *n* = noun, *v* = verb, *pv* = phrasal verb, *prep* = preposition, *exp* = expression

Note: There is space for you to write other words you would like to learn.

Unit 1

advise *v* to tell someone they should do something
afford *v* to be able to buy; to have enough money for
apologise *v* to say you're sorry
arrive at school *v* to get to school, usually in the morning before classes start
attend classes *v* to go to lessons, usually at school
break up *pv* when classes finish and the holidays start
can't stand *v* to dislike something or someone very much
canteen *n* a restaurant in an office, factory or school
classroom *n* a place in a school where lessons take place
communicate *v* to share information with other people
concentrate *v* to think carefully about something you're doing, and nothing else
creative *adj* producing or using new, original ideas
decorate *v* to put paint and paper on the walls; to make something look attractive
disappointed *adj* unhappy because something wasn't as good as expected or didn't happen
dislike *v* to not like something
drama *n* a play in a theatre or on television or radio
eat a packed lunch *v* to take food from home to school to eat at lunchtime
encourage *v* to make someone more likely to do something by saying or doing positive things
enjoy *v* to get pleasure from something
e-pal *n* somebody you write to on the internet but haven't met
exchange *v* to give something to someone and receive something similar from them
fond of *adj* liking something a lot
get good grades *v* to do well at school; to get good marks
get rid of *pv* to throw something away or to give it to someone because you no longer want or need it
good at *adj*; successful; able to do something well
go on a school trip *v* to take part in a trip arranged by the school, usually to learn something
gym *n* a large room in a school with equipment for exercising

hand in homework *pv* to give work to your teacher
hate *v* to dislike a lot
impressed *adj* when you admire or respect someone or something
interested in *adj* wanting to give your attention to something and discover more about it
IT room *n* a place in a school with lots of computers where pupils learn about technology
join an after-school club *v* to become a member of a club that takes place when normal school lessons have finished
(quite) like *v* to enjoy or approve of something or someone (a little)
look forward to *pv* to feel happy and excited about something that is going to happen
love *v* to like a lot
perform *v* to entertain people by dancing, singing, acting or playing music
persuade *v* to make someone agree to do something by talking to them a lot about it
pitch *n* a sports area for sports like football, hockey and rugby
playground *n* an area outside a school where the pupils can play
reception *n* a place where visitors to a school go when they first arrive
recipe *n* a list of foods and a set of instructions telling you how to cook something
school hall *n* a large room in a school where lots of people can get together at one time
science lab *n* a classroom where science lessons (e.g. physics, chemistry, biology) can take place
sports field *n* an area outside a school where games and sports can be played and taught
strict *adj* someone or something that makes sure other people behave themselves and don't break the rules
swimming pool *n* an area of water for swimming in
take exams *v* to do tests of knowledge or skill in various subjects
take up *pv* to start doing a particular activity or job
tennis court *n* a place to play tennis
wear a uniform *v* to wear a particular set of clothes, e.g. at school or in a particular job
work hard *v* to study a lot

Unit 2

achieve *v* to succeed in doing something difficult

ambition *n* a strong feeling that you want to be successful or powerful

athlete *n* someone who is good at sports such as running, jumping or throwing things

athletic *adj* strong, healthy and good at sports

athletics *n* a group of sports which include running, jumping and throwing

beat *v* to do something better than has been done before

believe in *pv* to feel confident that you or a person is good or right

champion *n* someone who has won an important sports competition

championship *n* a competition to find the best player or team in a sport

competition *n* a situation in which someone is trying to win something or be more successful than someone else

competitive *adj* wanting very much to win or be more successful than other people

competitor *n* someone who takes part in a sports competition

defeat *v* to win against someone in a fight or competition

disappointment *n* the feeling of being disappointed

diving *n* the activity or sport of jumping into water with your arms and head going in first

event *n* one of a set of races or competitions

fail *v* to not be successful

get in *pv* to succeed in entering a place, especially a building

give in *pv* to accept that you have been beaten and agree to stop competing or fighting

gymnast *n* a person who competes in gymnastics competitions

gymnastics *n* a sport, sometimes involving equipment, which shows how strong a person is and how easily they can move

have a positive/negative attitude *exp* to have good/bad opinions or feelings about something

join in *pv* to become involved in an activity with other people

lose *v* If you lose a game, the team or person that you are playing against wins.

luck *n* good and bad things caused by chance and not by your own actions

match *n* a sports competition or event in which two people or teams compete against each other

polite *adj* behaving in a way that is not rude and shows that you think about other people

respect *n* when you are polite to someone, especially because they are older or more important than you

rude *adj* behaving in a way which is not polite

score *v* to get points in a game or test
 n the number of points achieved in a game or test

stay in *pv* to stay in your home

succeed *v* to do something that you have been trying to do

talent *n* a natural ability to do something

win *v* to get the most points or succeed in a competition

Wordlist

Unit 3

bracelet *n* a piece of jewellery that you wear around your wrist or arm

button *n* a small, round object used to fasten clothing, such as a shirt or coat

casual *adj* Casual clothes are comfortable and not formal.

changing room *n* a room in a shop where you can try on clothes

collar *n* the part of a shirt or coat that is folded over and goes around your neck

comfortable *adj* Comfortable clothes give you a pleasant feeling and do not give you any problems.

cotton *adj* cloth made from the fibres of the cotton plant

cream *adj* a yellowish-white colour

dark (green) *adj* nearer to black than white in colour

definitely *adv* without any doubt

delayed *adj* happening at a later time than expected or intended

department store *n* a large shop that sells a lot of different types of thing

dress *n* a piece of clothing that covers the top half of the body and has a skirt that hangs down over the legs
v to wear clothes

earrings *n* jewellery worn on the ears

end up *pv* to be in a place or condition because of doing something

familiar *adj* easy to recognise because you've seen, met or heard it before

fashionable *adj* popular at a particular time

forbidden *adj* not allowed by a rule

gloves *n* clothing worn on the hands to keep them warm

gold *n* a valuable yellow metal that is used to make coins and jewellery
adj with the colour of gold

heel *n* the part of a shoe that is under the back of your foot

iron *n* a heavy hot object used to make clothes smooth

jacket *n* a short coat

jeans *n* trousers made of denim (= strong cotton cloth), usually worn informally

jumper *n* a piece of clothing made of wool that covers the arms and upper part of the body

leather *n* a material made from animal skin

light (blue) *adj* pale

location *n* a place or position

market *n* an outdoor place where you can buy lots of different things

material *n* cloth used for making clothes

maximum *n* the largest in amount, size or number that is allowed

navy blue *adj* dark blue

necklace *n* a piece of jewellery that you wear around your neck

online *adj* on the internet

pink *adj* a colour made by mixing red and white

purple *adj* a colour made by mixing red and blue

request *v* to ask someone to do something in a polite way

ring *n* a piece of jewellery that you wear on your finger

sandals *n* shoes with open toes you wear in the summer

second-hand *adj* something that someone else has owned or used before you

sew *v* to join things together with a needle and thread

shirt *n* a piece of clothing worn on the upper part of the body that usually has a collar and buttons on the front

silver *n* a valuable grey metal that is used to make coins and jewellery
adj with the colour of silver

skirt *n* a piece of clothing that hangs from the waist and does not have legs

sleeve *n* the part of a jacket, shirt, etc. that covers your arms

smart *adj* having a clean, tidy and stylish appearance

stylish *adj* attractive and fashionable

suit *n* a jacket and trousers, or a jacket and skirt, that are made from the same material
v to look good on someone

sweatshirt *n* a piece of casual clothing with long sleeves, usually made of thick cotton and worn on the upper part of the body

top *n* a piece of clothing worn on the upper part of the body

traditional *adj* following ways of behaving that have continued without changing for a long time

trainers *n* light, comfortable shoes, often worn for doing sport

T-shirt *n* a short-sleeved piece of clothing with no collar worn on the upper body

wool *n* a material made from the hair that grows on sheep

Unit 4

afraid (of) *adj* frightened or worried
amazed (about/by) *adj* very surprised
annoyed (about/by/with) *adj* angry
anxious (about) *adj* worried and nervous
audience *n* the people who watch a show/film
calm *adj* relaxed and quiet
challenging *adj* difficult, in a way that tests your ability
character *n* a person in a story
clap *v* to hit your hands together again and again at the end of a play or match to show you enjoyed it
comedy *n* a funny film or play
concert *n* a performance of music and singing
costume *n* the clothes an actor wears for a performance
deal with *v* to manage a situation
disappointed (about/by/with) *adj* unhappy because something didn't happen or something wasn't as you expected
excited (about/by) *adj* feeling very happy and interested
experience *n* something that happens to you
 v If you experience something, it happens to you or you feel it.
festival *n* a series of special events or performances
hero *n* a brave person who does good things
impressed (by/with) *adj* You are impressed by someone or something that you admire or respect.
jealous (of) *adj* not happy because someone else is better at something or has something you want
nervous *adj* worried or anxious
ordinary *adj* not special
power *n* a special ability
relax *v* to be calm and not worried
rely on *pv* to trust
satisfied (with) *adj* pleased with something you have done
science-fiction *adj* stories about life in the future or in other parts of the universe
serious (about) *adj* meaning what you say; not making a joke
shy *adj* not feeling confident
surprised (about/by) *adj* feeling surprise because something has happened that you did not expect
take part *pv* to be involved in an activity with other people
take place *pv* to happen
talent show *n* a concert where people with special abilities or skills are invited to perform, and sometimes compete for a prize
worried (about/by) *adj* unhappy because you are thinking about bad things that might happen

Wordlist

Unit 5

allowed *adj* have permission to do something

beef *n* the meat from a cow

boiled *adj* cooked in hot water

bread *n* a food made from flour, water and usually yeast, mixed together and baked

butter *n* a pale yellow food that is made from cream and is eaten on bread or used in cooking

cabbage *n* a large round hard green vegetable with lots of leaves that you eat raw or cooked

carrot *n* a long pointed orange vegetable

cheese *n* a food made from milk that can be either firm or soft and is usually yellow or white

chicken *n* a type of bird kept on a farm for its eggs, or the meat from this bird that is cooked and eaten

cod *n* a type of fish

corn *n* a long vegetable made up of lots of yellow seeds

fish *n* an animal that lives in water and breathes by taking water in through its mouth. It is often caught and eaten as food.

fit *adj* healthy and strong, especially as a result of exercise

fitness *n* the condition of being strong and healthy

fried *adj* cooked in hot oil or fat

frozen *adj* frozen food is very cold and has been frozen so that it will last a long time

fruit *n* the soft part containing seeds that is produced by a plant. Many types of fruit are sweet and can be eaten.

grape *n* a small round purple or pale green fruit that you can eat or make into wine

health *n* the condition of the body and the degree to which it is free from illness

healthy *adj* making you strong and not ill

label *n* a small piece of paper or other material with information on it

lamb *n* a young sheep; the meat from a baby sheep

lettuce *n* a green vegetable with lots of soft green leaves that you use in salads

peach *n* a fruit that has a soft skin and is yellow/pink and has a yellow inside with a large seed

permit *v* to allow something

pineapple *n* a fruit that grows in hot countries and is large and yellow with a thick yellow-brown skin with sharp points on it

put away *pv* to put something in its usual place

put down *pv* to write someone's name on a list to include them in an event; to put something you are carrying somewhere (e.g. on a table)

put off *pv* to delay doing something

put on *pv* to switch on (e.g. a light); to increase (e.g. weight); to wear

put out *pv* to switch off (e.g. a light); to make a fire stop burning

put up *pv* to increase (e.g. prices)

raw *adj* not cooked

require *v* If a rule requires something, you must do that thing.

responsible *adj* in charge of someone or something

salad *n* a mixture of raw vegetables, usually including lettuce, eaten either as a separate dish or with other food

salmon *n* a large fish which is pink when it is cooked

soup *n* a usually hot liquid food made from vegetables, meat or fish

spinach *n* a green vegetable with dark green leaves that are cooked or eaten raw in salads

strawberry *n* a small soft red fruit with lots of seeds on the outside

tuna *n* a type of fish

turkey *n* a large bird like a chicken

unfit *adj* not healthy because you do too little exercise

unhealthy *adj* not good for your health; not strong and well

yoghurt *n* a food made from milk that is thick and a bit sour (= not sweet)

Unit 6

art gallery *n* a public building where people can look at works of art

balcony *n* an area with a wall or bars around it that is joined to the outside wall of a building on an upper level

beach *n* an area of sand or small stones near the sea or another area of water such as a lake

castle *n* a large strong building, built in the past by a ruler or important person to protect the people inside from attack

city *n* a large town

coast *n* the land next to the sea

concentrate *v* to think carefully about only what you're doing and nothing else

convenient *adj* near or easy to get to

cosy *adj* comfortable and warm

countryside *n* land not in towns or cities that is either used for farming or left in its natural condition

crowded *adj* If a place is crowded, it is full of people.

cultural events *npl* Exhibitions, films and concerts are examples of cultural events.

desert *n* an area often covered with sand or rocks where there is very little rain and not many plants

dull *adj* boring

forest *n* a large area of land covered with trees and plants, usually larger than a wood

freezing *adj* extremely cold

historical building *n* a building connected with the past

huge *adj* extremely large

island *n* a piece of land completely surrounded by water

jungle *n* an area of land in a hot country where trees and plants grow close together

ladder *n* a thing you climb up when you want to reach a high place. It has two long vertical pieces joined together by lots of shorter horizontal pieces.

lake *n* a large area of water surrounded by land and not connected to the sea except by rivers or streams

lively *adj* A lively person or place is full of energy and interest.

mountain *n* a raised part of the Earth, larger than a hill

peaceful *adj* quiet and calm

sociable *adj* A sociable person likes being with people and meeting new people.

space *n* an empty area that is available to be used

storm *n* very bad weather with a lot of rain, snow, wind, etc.

view *n* what you can see from a particular place

village *n* a group of houses and other buildings that is smaller than a town, usually in the countryside

Wordlist

Unit 7

bat *n* a small animal like a mouse with wings that flies at night

cage *n* a space surrounded on all sides by wire or metal bars, used for keeping birds or animals in

calm *adj* If the weather or the sea is calm, it is quiet and peaceful.

camel *n* a large animal that lives in hot, dry places and has one or two humps (= raised parts on its back)

clear *adj* If the sky is clear, there are no clouds.

climate change *n* the way the Earth's weather is changing

cruel *adj* very unkind, or causing pain to people or animals intentionally

elephant *n* a very large, grey animal with big ears and a very long nose

environment *n* the natural world including the land, water, air, plants and animals

frozen *adj* turned into ice

gorilla *n* a big, black, hairy animal, like a large monkey

humid *adj* Humid air or weather is hot and a bit wet.

ice *n* water that has frozen and become solid

keep (doing) *v* to continue doing something

litter *n* pieces of paper and other waste that are left in public places

ocean *n* one of the five main areas of sea

oil *n* a thick liquid which comes from under the Earth's surface and which is used as a fuel

parrot *n* a colourful bird which lives in hot countries and which can copy what people say

penguin *n* a large black and white sea bird that swims and cannot fly

pollution *n* damage caused to water, air, etc. by bad substances or waste

protect *v* to keep someone or something safe from something dangerous or bad

rare *adj* very unusual

recycling *n* when paper, glass, plastic, etc. is put through a process so that it can be used again

river *n* a long, natural area of water that flows across the land

shark *n* a large fish with very sharp teeth

snake *n* a long, thin creature with no legs that slides along the ground

species *n* a group of animals from the same family

spider *n* a creature with eight long legs which catches insects in a web (= structure like a net)

sunset *n* when the sun disappears in the evening and the sky becomes dark

tiger *n* a large wild cat that has yellow fur with black lines on it

waterfall *n* a stream of water that falls from a high place, often to a pool below

whale *n* a very large animal that looks like a large fish and lives in the sea

wildlife *n* animals, birds and plants in the place where they live

Unit 8

airport *n* a place where planes regularly take off and land, with buildings for passengers to wait in

ambition *n* something you would like to achieve

boarding pass *n* a card that a passenger must have to be allowed to get on a plane or a ship

check in *v* to show your ticket at an airport so that you can be told where you will be sitting and so that your bags can be put on the plane

gate *n* a part of an airport where passengers are allowed to get on or off a plane

harbour *n* an area of water near the coast where ships are kept

influence *v* to affect or change how someone or something develops, behaves or thinks

land *v* to arrive on the ground after flying through the air

motorway *n* a wide road for fast-moving traffic

pilot *n* a person who flies a plane

platform *n* the area in a railway station where you get on and off the train

rough *adj* not even or smooth; with big waves

roundabout *n* a place where three or more roads join; traffic must go around an area in the middle

seat belt *n* a belt that you wear in a car, bus, plane, etc. that protects you in case of an accident

security *n* the area of a building (e.g. an airport) where people are checked to make sure they are not carrying anything dangerous

selfie *n* a photo you take of yourself, e.g. with your mobile phone

slightly *adv* a little

station *n* a place where buses or trains stop for people to get on or off

stuff *n* a word we use to talk about things without saying exactly what they are

submarine *n* a boat that travels under the water

take off *pv* to leave the ground and begin to fly

traffic jam *n* a line of cars, trucks, etc. that are moving slowly or not at all

traffic lights *n* a set of red, yellow and green lights that control the movement of traffic

wave *n* a raised line of water that moves across the sea

weigh *v* to measure how heavy someone or something is

Acknowledgements

Author acknowledgements

Sue Elliot and Amanda Thomas would both like to thank each other as co-authors, and would also like to extend their thanks to their families for all their help and support.

Publishers acknowledgements

The authors and publishers are grateful and would like to extend a special thanks to Lorraine Poulter, Sarah Dev-Sherman (Project Manager – for holding everything together so brilliantly), Catriona Watson-Brown (Editor – for her sterling work in managing the proof stages), Leon Chambers (Audio Producer), Soundhouse studios and Wild Apple Design.

In addition, the publishers and authors would like to thank the following for their role in reviewing the material in general and in particular those who participated in the development of the exam tasks: Jane Coates, Sara Georgina Vargas Ochoa, Cressida Hicks, Judy Alden, Annie Broadhead, Tom Bradbury, Sarah Dymond, Mark Little, Marla Del Signore, Bartosz Michalowski, Catriona Watson-Brown, Alison Sharpe, Sheila Thorn, Lucy Mordini, Trish Chapman, Sarah Curtis.

Development of this publication has made use of the Cambridge English Corpus (CEC). The CEC is a computer database of contemporary spoken and written English, which currently stands at over one billion words. It includes British English, American English and other varieties of English. It also includes the Cambridge Learner corpus, developed in collaboration with the University of Cambridge ESOL examinations. Cambridge University Press has built up the CEC in order to provide evidence of authentic language use to better inform the production of learning materials.

This product is also informed by English Profile, a collaborative programme designed to enhance the learning, teaching and assessment of English worldwide. Its main partners are Cambridge University Press and Cambridge ESOL exams and its aim is create a profile for English usage based on the Common European Framework of Reference for Languages (CEFR). English Profile outcomes, such as the English Vocabulary Profile provide detailed information based on language level and help inform the language that learners can be expected to demonstrate at each CEFR level, offering a clear benchmark for learner's proficiency. For more information, please visit www.englishprofile.org.

The authors and publishers acknowledge the following sources of copyright material and are grateful for the permissions granted. While every effort has been made, it has not always been possible to identify the sources of all the material used, or to trace all copyright holders. If any omissions are brought to our notice, we will be happy to include the appropriate acknowledgements on reprinting and in the next update to the digital edition, as applicable.

Key: U = Unit, GR = Grammar reference, PVB = Phrasal verb builder, SB = Speaking bank

Photography

The following images are sourced from Getty Images.

U1: Celso Mollo Photography/Moment Open; Ittipol Nampochai/EyeEm; Vijay kumar/DigitalVision Vectors; Steve Debenport/E+; Layland Masuda/Moment Open; Gary John Norman/DigitalVision; studerga/iStock/Getty Images Plus; Juanmonino/iStock/Getty Images Plus; Ron Levine/DigitalVision; Axelle/Bauer-Griffin/FilmMagic; Lance King/Getty Images Sport; Juice Images; Alistair Berg/DigitalVision; U2: Photo Graphic Com/Corbis Sport; Emmanuel Dunand/AFP; Carl De Souza/AFP; Eric Feferberg/AFP; Chris Ryan/Caiaimage; Tim de Waele/Corbis Sport; Visionhaus/Corbis Sport; Adie Bush/Cultura; Tim Clayton/Corbis Sport; Emilija Manevska/

Moment; Alys Tomlinson/Taxi; U3: lechatnoir/E+; John Lund/Marc Romanelli/Blend Images; Tony Anderson/ The Image Bank; Yellow Dog Productions/DigitalVision; Maica/E+; Linh Ho/EyeEm; Flashpop/Iconica; U4: yogysic/DigitalVision Vectors; nicolecioe/DigitalVision Vectors; Mike Kemp; Gardiner Anderson/Bauer-Griffin/ GC Images; Robert Daly/OJO Images; Chris Whitehead/Cultura; moodboard/Cultura; fotog; arabianEye; Simon Battensby/Photographer's Choice; U5: sanjeri/E+; Stefan Christmann/Corbis Documentary; Bob Thomas/ DigitalVision; Birgid Allig/Stockbyte; Gareth Morgans/StockFood Creative; Johner Images; Alex Ortega/ EyeEm; manaemedia/iStock/Getty Images Plus; Astrakan Images/Cultura; U6: IIC/Axiom/Perspectives; Dennis Gilbert/Corbis Documentary; TuiPhotoengineer/iStock/Getty Images Plus; Spaces Images/Blend Images; Thomas Northcut/DigitalVision; Jim Jordan Photography/Photographer's Choice; Visions Of Our Land/The Image Bank; Thanapol Tontinikorn/Moment; QQ7/iStock/Getty Images Plus; W. Buss/De Agostini Picture Library; somchaisom/iStock/Getty Images Plus; Blend Images - KidStock/Brand X Pictures; U7: PeopleImages/ E+; John Hart/EyeEm; Henn Photography/Cultura; JanRoode/iStock/Getty Images Plus; Juanmonino/E+; Stígur Már Karlsson/Heimsmyndir/E+; Westend61; SoumenNath/E+; Huerta, Anna; Jonathan & Angela Scott/ AWL Images; mikroman6/Moment; R A Kearton/Moment Open; U8: Image Source; Chris_Fisher/iStock/Getty Images Plus; Gail Shotlander/Moment; Carlos Davila/Photographer's Choice; Jbryson/iStock/Getty Images Plus; Image Source; Kevin Peterson/Photodisc; Daniel Viñé Garcia/Moment; Oscar Bjarnason/Cultura; levente bodo/Moment; Karl Weatherly/Photodisc; possum1961/iStock Editorial/Getty Images Plus; Robert Niedring/ Alloy; Nick Daly/Cultura; Erik Isakson; freemixer/E+; Mark Ralston/AFP; GR: majorosl/iStock/Getty Images Plus; Jeff Greenberg/Universal Images Group; funky-data/iStock/Getty Images Plus; onurdongel/iStock/Getty Images Plus; Pekka Sakki/AFP; kali9/iStock/Getty Images Plus; Andersen Ross/Stockbyte; Mlenny/E+; Michael Dunning/Photographer's Choice; amanaimagesRF; Pola Damonte/Moment; Newton Daly/DigitalVision; Plush Studios/Bill Reitzel/Blend Images; SolStock/E+; repinanatoly/iStock/Getty Images Plus; GavinD/E+; Juice Images; Pilar Snchez/EyeEm; SB: NoSystem images/E+; Hero Images; Ronnie Kaufman/Larry Hirshowitz/Blend Images; Hero Images; Caiaimage/Chris Ryan; Ronnie Kaufman/Larry Hirshowitz/Blend Images; filadendron/ E+; Henn Photography; Juice Images; PVB: Alistair Berg/DigitalVision; fotog; Emilija Manevska/Moment; TuiPhotoengineer/iStock/Getty Images Plus.

The below image has been sourced from Shutterstock.
U7: Sura Nualpradid/Shutterstock

Front cover photography by William King/The Image Bank/Getty Images; Sir Francis Canker Photography/ Moment/Getty Images; vladj55/iStock/Getty Images Plus/Getty Images; fitopardo.com/Moment/Getty Images; EnginKorkmaz/iStock Editorial/Getty Images Plus/Getty Images; Laurie Noble/DigitalVision/Getty Images; Pawel Toczynski/Photographer's Choice/Getty Images.

Illustration
Jo and Alina from KJA Agency; Giuliano Aloisi from Advocate Art.

Audio
Audio recordings by Leon Chambers. Recorded at Soundhouse Studios, London.